The Way to the Kingdom

Written by TIM REEVE
Illustrated by DIANA CATCHPOLE

This is number *Proof copy A3* of a limited signed edition of 1,500 copies

Tim Reeve

A guide to the Bible and to Prayer for all age-groups – written as a drama, with dialogue from the Scriptures – containing 77 full-colour illustrations and commentary based on advice of clergy from four Christian denominations.

First Published by Ferard-Reeve Publishing Ltd 1991
Greenfields Farmhouse, Kings Barn Lane, Steyning, Sussex, BN44 3YG

Presentation Edition June 1991

Typeset in England by Rowland Phototypesetting Ltd
Bury St Edmunds, Suffolk

Printed in Hong Kong by Colocraft Ltd

British Library Catalogue in Publication Data
Reeve, Tim
    The way to the kingdom: a guide to the
    Bible and to prayer for all age groups.
    1 Christianity. Scriptures
    220.61

ISBN 0 9517017 0 3

Contents

A Prayer for Confirmation Day

May you take comfort from the hands that lay their blessing on your head this day;
And when they bring the bread and wine, remember that unbroken line
Of all the blessing hands that reach right back to His, Who came to teach and
sacrificed His life to give mankind – through grace and truth – a chance to live.

AUTHOR'S PRAYER

Author's Preface and Summary of the Book

I designed and wrote this book originally for my grandchildren and godchildren. I wanted to fulfil the promises made at their baptisms to ensure that they grew up to understand the Bible. I also hoped that the book would appeal to them in different ways at all ages.

The design of the book is not unlike one of those illustrated 'Books of Hours' produced in the Middle Ages for use in those periods during the day that were set aside for private devotion – the Canonical Hours – from Matins and Lauds to Vespers and Compline.

The book contains two main sections: Part One, the Bible, presented as a drama with commentary, using quotations from the Scriptures as dialogue to give the main spiritual messages and stories: Part Two, an illustrated guide to prayer from the earliest days of the Church until modern times. This part ends with an Epilogue on the universal church in relation to the other great world faiths.

The Bible section contains over 600 quotations from the Scriptures, spoken by the main biblical characters and linked together by a Story-Teller and an Interpreter. This takes up fifty-two scenes – one for each week of the year – and includes a scene on the Apocrypha. This forms a continuous drama in narrative form, which is not much longer than some Shakespeare plays.

I hope the illustrations will appeal to young children and that parents and others will be able to tell them the stories, using the text as a basis, while they look at the pictures. The text is designed more for those who are being prepared for their Confirmation and also for adults who may wish to renew or review their faith later in life.

Throughout the work on the book, I have been helped by the advice and criticism of seven priests and ministers from the Anglican, Roman Catholic, Methodist and Baptist Churches. I acknowledge their help below.

I showed the draft manuscript to Dr Robert Runcie, now Lord Runcie, when he was Archbishop of Canterbury. He told me that the book moved him very much. He encouraged me to publish the book and gave me permission to print and illustrate his prayer, 'Grant us Reverence for Life', as his contribution to the work.

I hope that the book and the pictures will be both enjoyable and memorable and encourage further reading from the Bible, so, perhaps, turning seeing into believing.

TIM REEVE
MARCH 1991

Acknowledgements

I acknowledge with gratitude the help I have received from so many people and from so many sources – especially:–

His Royal Highness, the Prince of Wales KG, for giving me permission to quote from one of his speeches (see page 130).

The Right Reverend and Right Honourable Dr Robert Runcie PC MC DD, Lord Runcie of Cuddesdon, Archbishop of Canterbury 1980–1991, for discussing with me the original manuscript of the book at Lambeth Palace and for allowing me to publish his prayer 'Grant us Reverence for Life', and for his encouragement.

The seven priests and ministers, of four different Christian denominations, who helped me with their advice and criticism:–

The Revd Roy Boff MA, Rector of Romaldkirk in the diocese of Ripon; The Revd Peter Burch FCA, Vicar of St Andrew's, Steyning, Sussex, in the diocese of Chichester; Father Gerald Coates of the Roman Catholic Church of Christ the King, Steyning; The Revd Edward Hiscox MA, Rector of Duntisbourne Abbots, in the diocese of Gloucester; the Revd Barbara Heather, Baptist Minister at 'Barrswood', Groombridge, Sussex; The Revd Douglas Hopwood, Methodist Minister of Storrington and Steyning; The Revd Basil Watson OBE MA RN, Chaplain to the Worshipful Company of Girdlers in the City of London and former Vicar of St Lawrence, Jewry.

The many friends and helpers who have read the early drafts of the manuscript and given me invaluable suggestions:–

Alan Bailey of ABS Communications, London, my editor; my former partner in Kenya, the late Wing Commander Graham Boswell OBE RAF and his widow, Erica Boswell; Général Hervé Burin des Roziers, Chevalier of the Legion of Honour, Croix de Guerre, of Versailles; the late Gwen Catchpole; Rosemary Chamberlin; George Cockman, Assistant Headmaster of Steyning Grammar School; The Rt Hon. The Lord Crathorne DL; Senator William Flowers of Georgia USA; Patrick Hinton; Col. Robert Hornby, OBE, Secretary of the Farmington Trust for religious education, Oxford; Dudley J. Hughes of Jackson, Mississippi, USA; Innes and Rosemary Innes-Watson; His Honour Christopher Lea MC; Charles MacDonald, Organist, St Andrew's, Steyning; Professor Keith and Susan Middlemas; John and 'Mops' Millard-Barnes; Lieutenant Bede Northcote RN; John Stevens; the late Hugh Sisam; Sir Richard Temple, Bart. MC and Lady Temple; Richard Temple of The Temple Gallery, London; Anthony Veale, the artist, and his wife, Susan.

I wish to thank the religious affairs correspondent of 'The Times' newspaper, Clifford Longley, whose weekly articles have inspired and guided me throughout the past seven years and have had a great influence on this work.

Messrs Hodder & Stoughton and Tony Castle for giving me permission to reproduce their translations and versions of the prayers from the Hodder Book of Christian Prayers (Copyright 1986); also the SCM Press Ltd for permission to print the prayer from their book Dietrich Bonhoeffer, 'Letters and Papers from Prison', The Enlarged Edition, SCM Press 1971. Extracts from 'We Believe in God', a Report by the Doctrine Commission of the Church of England (Church House Publishing 1986), are reproduced by permission of the Central Board of Finance of the Church of England. This report has been invaluable.

Finally, I must thank Diana Catchpole for the way she has turned my rough cartoons into the pictures presented here. Also, I could not have finished this work without the love, support, encouragement and advice of my wife, Penelope, of my four children and stepdaughter and the help and skill of Victoria Mitchell, Maria Munoz and Beverley Waldron, who have prepared the book for the printers and binders.

TIM REEVE
MARCH 1991

Part One
The Bible as a Drama

'The sacred writings of Judaism and Christianity are probably the most influential collection of books in human history.'

From the Encyclopaedia Britannica

Saint Jerome, Translator of the Bible

STORY-TELLER: We start with this picture of St Jerome since, without him, many of the most famous phrases in the Bible might have been written quite differently.

Jerome was sent to Bethlehem in Palestine, or what is now called Israel, in the year 386 AD by Pope Damasus, to make a reliable translation of the Bible into Latin. He spent most of the rest of his life completing this great task. All other translations of the Bible since then have been based on Jerome's work.

Jerome lived from about 342–420 AD. He had been the Pope's secretary and was a great scholar. At Bethlehem, he lived in a monastery with a team of scholars. They translated the Sacred Scriptures from the Hebrew, Aramaic and Greek of the oldest documents available to them. They were financed by a rich Roman matron known to us as St Paula.

Although Jerome's robes seem like those of a cardinal of the Church, this is not the case. He is robed as a Doctor of the Church – the College of Cardinals was not created until 1069. We include the lion in the picture as Jerome's companion since this was the way he was usually painted from the earliest representations of him. There are many legends to account for the presence of the lion. However, the real reason for his being shown as Jerome's traditional companion may more probably be due to an attempt to show one of his chief attributes – fierceness towards all documents that he thought were spurious or heretical. The lion is, therefore, included here as a guarantor of Jerome's integrity as a scholar.

Now let us turn to the first picture of a Bible scene, from the first words in the Book of Genesis. This shows the very moment at the beginning of time when God made heaven and earth – the Creation.

In the beginning | God created the Heaven | And the earth

OLD TESTAMENT SCENE 1   *The Creation of the Universe*   Approximate geological time:
(Genesis 1)   10–15,000 plus million years ago[1]

STORY-TELLER: *In the beginning, God created the heavens and the earth. The earth was without form and void, and darkness was upon the face of the deep; and the Spirit of God was moving over the face of the waters.*

VOICE OF GOD: *'Let there be light!'*

STORY-TELLER: *And there was light. And God separated the light from the darkness. God called the light Day and the darkness he called Night.*

VOICE OF GOD: *'Let the waters under the heavens be gathered into one place and let dry land appear.'*

STORY-TELLER: *And God made two great lights, the greater light to rule the day and the lesser light to rule the night. And God set them in the canopy of the heavens to give light upon the earth. He made the stars also.*

INTERPRETER: We illustrate 'creation' as a vast explosion in space. Most Christian scholars have recognised – since the mid-20th century – that the biblical moment of creation with the coming of 'light' is matched by the 'big bang' theory put forward by scientists. This scientific theory is attractive to believers. It implies that an outside hand – the Hand of God – caused the original tiny particle of matter to be exploded.

Scientists like Professor Stephen Hawking[2] feel the need to pursue their theories still further. They need to be able to say what the universe really is in scientific terms. They have already advanced from the original 'big bang' theory and some suggest – through the theory of quantum physics – that there are mathematical grounds for showing that there may be a conscious reality at the heart of the universe. This ultimate reality – if they prove it – would seem to be indistinguishable from God.

STORY-TELLER: Science can help interpret, but belief in God does not depend on scientific proof. It depends on faith. Faith can come through inspired observation or intuition – as in this story from Genesis. Faith can come through reason or the feeling that we are not only just brain and body but also have a spirit. It is through this spirit that faith comes as revelation. Since time immemorial, it made mankind aware of a Being outside and beyond themselves and this material universe. The Bible records one great people's spiritual experiences of this Being – worshipped as God. The saints, religious heroes and countless ordinary people also record spiritual experiences ever since biblical times.

INTERPRETER: The problem with these experiences – whether of visions, 'voices', 'signs' or even direct revelations – is that mortal minds cannot comprehend fully the mind of the infinite. Not everyone can believe all the interpretations put on their visions by the prophets. Yet they can be brought into better focus if we regard them as part of a slowly-developing picture of the nature of God, his purpose for us and the way we should live.

STORY-TELLER: Theologians must try to interpret all this to each new generation in terms it can understand. Yet, like scientists, they too still stand before immense mysteries. If theologians, scientists, philosophers and others can work together to interpret the spiritual implications of new discoveries, then millions more may find they can believe in 'God the Father, maker of heaven and earth' – thus ushering in a New Age of Faith.

[1]We put 'geological time' here and for the next scene because that is the nearest our scientists can estimate the periods of creation of life and the universe. Nevertheless, we recognise that, in relation to God, time does not exist, for God is Eternal, he has no 'Beginning' in our sense, he is timeless. As we shall see, this is crucial to the Christian understanding of God, for Jesus, whom we shall see is God Incarnate – God made flesh – only has a 'Beginning' in the sense that he took human form. This is why we shall see him say: *'Before Abraham was I AM'* (John 8/58) and also *'I and the Father are one'* (John 10/30) and why he is described by St John (1/3) and St Paul (Hebrews 1/2) as the AGENT of creation.
[2]Professor Stephen N. Hawking CH CBE, FRS, Lucasian Professor of Mathematics at Cambridge University. See his book 'A Brief History of Time' (from the Big Bang to the Black Holes), Bantam Press 1988.

Let the earth bring forth grass and the fruit tree

God created the great sea monsters and all kinds of birds

And God said—let us make man in our own image

OLD TESTAMENT SCENE 2   *The Creation of Life on Earth*   Geological time: from *c.* 1,500 million

(Genesis 1)   to 2 million BC

VOICE OF GOD: *'Let the Earth put forth vegetation, plants yielding seed and fruit-trees bearing fruit. Let the waters bring swarms of living creatures and let birds fly above the earth across the canopy of heaven.'*

STORY-TELLER: *So God created the great sea-monsters and every living creature that moves, with which the waters swarm, and every winged bird. And God saw that it was good. And God said:*

VOICE OF GOD: *'Let the Earth bring forth living creatures: cattle and creeping things and beasts of the earth.'*

STORY-TELLER: *And it was so. And God saw that it was good.*

VOICE OF GOD: *'Let us make man in our own image, after our likeness; and let them have dominion over the fish of the sea, and over the birds of the air, and over the cattle and over all the earth.'*

STORY-TELLER: *So God created Man in his own image, in the image of God he created him; male and female he created them. And God blessed them:*

VOICE OF GOD: *'Be fruitful and multiply, and fill the Earth and subdue it.'*

STORY-TELLER: *And God saw everything that he had made and behold it was very good.*

INTERPRETER: The story also tells us that God took only six days over all his creation and that, on the seventh day, he rested, making it a holy day. Although we know that this seems to concertina time, it does not say that the six days of creation were consecutive – more like periods of creation. In those far off days, there was no 'Time' in the way we know it now. For countless ages, the Universe was ablaze, bright with molten lava and glowing gasses taking form. Time was measured – in retrospect – in ages, not in years or days. We sing of this in the hymn that contains these words: *'A thousand ages in thy sight are like an evening gone'*.

There is no way of telling whether the Hebrew priests, who first wrote this story some 3,000 years ago, were conscious of this notion or of the fact that God's creative process is still continuing, as the universe expands. But it is remarkable that, in their account of the creation of Life, they should visualise the different forms of life coming into being in exactly the same order as our scientists have since proved to have been the case – first grasses – then fish – then reptiles and birds and so on, with mankind being the last to be created.

Their story, therefore, written down after it had been passed only by word of mouth for many generations, is not just a myth, as some have declared it to be. For example, even if we look for God within our new physics – the quantum theory – where human consciousness mirrors that of reality's ultimate ground, it makes sense to speak of human beings being created in God's image. Those Hebrew priests, therefore, were right to think of us as partners in God's new kingdom, or as stewards, to take care of his creation and not to abuse it.

Adam and Eve

Adam & Eve were naked & unashamed   Ye shall become as Gods   God sent them forth

OLD TESTAMENT SCENE 3   *The Story of Adam & Eve in the Garden of Eden*   Time: After *c.* 2 million years ago

(Genesis 2–4)

INTERPRETER: After describing the creation of life, the Book of Genesis gives a second description to enlarge the first – this focusses on actual people like ourselves, Adam and Eve, the first man and woman.[1] They were people to whom God could communicate (through his Holy Spirit) and who were capable of appreciating his moral and spiritual laws. The scriptures read as follows:

STORY-TELLER: *Then the LORD God formed man of dust from the ground and breathed into his nostrils the breath of life: and man became a living being. And the LORD God planted a garden in Eden in the East; there he put the man he had formed. And the LORD commanded him saying:*

VOICE OF GOD: *'You may eat freely of every tree in the garden; but of the tree of knowledge of good and evil you shall not eat, for in the day that you eat it you shall surely die.'*

STORY-TELLER: *Then the LORD God said: 'it is not good that man should be alone; I will make a helper fit for him'.*

God caused a deep sleep to fall upon the man. Then he took one of his ribs and formed it into a woman and brought her to him. *They became one flesh and were both naked and unashamed.* But a serpent in the garden told the woman that if she and Adam ate the forbidden fruit they would not die, but instead . . .

SERPENT: *'You will be like gods, knowing good and evil.'*

STORY-TELLER: So the woman ate the fruit and shared it with Adam. *Then the eyes of both were opened and they knew that they were naked; they sewed fig-leaves together and made themselves aprons. And they heard the sound of the LORD God walking in the garden in the cool of the day, and the man and his wife hid themselves.* The LORD God then found them out and was angry at what they had done. He drove them out of Eden, saying

VOICE OF GOD: *'Cursed is the ground because of you. In the sweat of your face shall you eat bread till you return to the ground. Dust you are, and to dust you shall return.'*

INTERPRETER: This story brings us to the heart of the first moral and spiritual issue in the Bible – the development of conscience, that still small voice within us all. God gave mankind free-will – even the free-will to disobey him. The story shows that, if we do disobey – according to Genesis – and break God's moral laws, we shall suffer. The story pinpoints the strange fact that humankind prefers to do evil rather than good. Man 'fell' from the ideal (the Garden of Eden) – 'to err is human'. The Church calls this the doctrine of Original Sin, our natural bias against God.

As we go through the Scriptures from this chapter onwards, we shall find that the ideas of our relationship with God and of his nature become more complex. These Scriptures describe what is in effect a series of revelations. They illustrate a developing faith, which can be seen, first, through the Old Testament – which is a record of one very devout people's experience of God – and, finally, through direct revelation, when God came down to earth in the person of Jesus Christ.

[1] Adam comes from the Hebrew root-word meaning 'Mankind'; similarly Eve means 'Womankind' or 'Source of Life'.

Noah and the Flood

Noah found grace in the eyes of God   I do bring a flood   I set my bow in the cloud

OLD TESTAMENT SCENE 4

Noah and the Flood

(Genesis 5–10)

Time: Prehistoric, but
within folk memory

INTERPRETER: The story of Noah and the flood is recorded in Sumerian and Babylonian remains as well as by the Hebrews. It seems to have been a folk-memory of a vast prehistoric natural disaster. It is described in the Bible to show the primitive belief of the Hebrew priests that all disasters and suffering come from God as a punishment for sin. Later on, as we shall see, particularly in the book of Job, the writers of the Bible were not satisfied with this. They wanted to find out why the innocent also suffered pain and undeserved hardship.[1]

STORY-TELLER: Before telling the story, we need to fill the gap between Adam and Eve and the development of their descendants up to Noah's time. We show the image of Adam's son, Cain, killing his brother, Abel, to signify this passage of time. The scene is in the top left corner of the picture. Adam had a third son, Seth, from whom Noah was descended. It was in the time of Seth's grandson, Enosh, that, according to Genesis, *men first began to call upon the name of the LORD* – in other words, the start of true religion. However, despite this belief in God, men and women became increasingly wicked and Genesis describes how . . .

The LORD saw that the wickedness of man was great in the earth, and that every imagination of his heart was only evil continually. And the LORD was sorry that he had made man. So the LORD said:

VOICE OF GOD: *'I will blot out man whom I have created, man and beast, creeping things and birds of the air.'*

STORY-TELLER: *But Noah found favour in the eyes of the LORD. Noah was a righteous man, blameless in his generation. Noah walked with God. And Noah had three sons, Ham, Shem and Japheth. God spoke to Noah:*

VOICE OF GOD: *'I have determined to make an end of all flesh; for the earth is filled with violence. Make an ark of gopher wood. For behold I bring a flood of waters to destroy all flesh. But you shall come into the ark, you, your sons, your wife, your sons' wives and of every living thing, two of every sort.'*

STORY-TELLER: Noah built the ark and went on board with his family and two each of every creature, male and female. The rain then came down for forty days and nights. All life outside the ark was drowned. Then *the fountains of the deep and the windows of heaven were closed*. The ark came to rest on Mount Ararat. The LORD told Noah to disembark with his family and all his live cargo. Then he said to Noah:

VOICE OF GOD: *'I will never again curse the ground because of man, for the imagination of man's heart is evil from his youth. Neither shall I destroy every living creature as I have done. This is the sign of the covenant between you and me and every living creature that is with you for all future generations: I set my bow in the cloud. When I bring clouds over the earth and the bow is in the clouds I will remember my covenant.'*

INTERPRETER: This story shows the Hebrew belief that God always tempers justice with mercy.

STORY-TELLER: Before going on to the next scene – of Abraham and the founding fathers of the Children of Israel – we must mention one well-known story that is told in Genesis immediately after Noah and the flood. This is the story of the Tower of Babel. First, after the flood, Noah's sons had families and from these the nations spread abroad on the earth. Later on, these peoples decided to build a tower, the Tower of Babel, designed to reach up to heaven so that they would *make a name* for themselves. Seeing their conceit and their pride in material things, the LORD prevented them from building any higher and over-reaching themselves and even trying to challenge God himself.

[1]It was only much later, when God considered that humankind had matured enough morally, that he sent Jesus to show us that, although doing evil brought punishment, evil could be overcome by love. He also gave us hope – which the Jews did not have at this stage – of a future life beyond their Sheol or Hades.

OLD TESTAMENT SCENE 5   *Abraham and the Forefathers of the Tribe of Israel*   *c.*2000–*c.*1,600 BC

(Genesis 11–50)

STORY-TELLER: We now come to the saga of Abraham and the Patriarchs, the traditional founders of the tribes of Israel. Abraham was descended from Noah's son, Shem.

VOICE OF GOD: *'I am God Almighty. Walk before me and be blameless. Fear not Abraham, I am your shield. I will make many nations for you. And I will give your descendants the land of Canaan for ever.'*[1]

STORY-TELLER: *After this God tested Abraham: he said to him:–*

VOICE OF GOD: *'Take your son, your only son Isaac, whom you love and offer him as a burnt sacrifice on the mountains.'*

STORY-TELLER: *So both of them went together. And Isaac said to Abraham:*

ISAAC: *'Father! Behold the fire and the wood, but where is the lamb for the burnt offering?'*

ABRAHAM: *'God will himself provide a lamb.'*

STORY-TELLER: *Then Abraham took his knife to slay his son. But the Angel of the Lord cried out from heaven:–*

ANGEL: *'Abraham! Do not lay your hands on the lad: for now I know you fear the LORD.'*

STORY-TELLER: *Abraham looked, and behind him there was a ram caught in a thicket. He offered it instead of Isaac.*

Many years later, God spoke to Isaac's son, Jacob. Jacob had cheated his brother, Esau, but had repented after he had seen, in a dream, the Lord standing on a ladder leading to heaven. The Lord told Jacob to *'Put away foreign gods and make an altar to the God who appeared to you when you fled from your brother Esau.*[2] Jacob did as he was told. Then God changed Jacob's name to ISRAEL and said: *'I am God Almighty, be fruitful and multiply and a nation of kings shall spring from you. The land which I gave to Abraham and Isaac I will give to you.'* Jacob then set up a pillar at Bethel, the place where God had spoken to him.

Now Jacob loved his son Joseph more than all his children and made him a coat of many colours.[3] *His brothers were jealous of him. They cast him into a pit. Traders passing by lifted Joseph from the pit and sold him to Egypt.* Some time later, Pharaoh, king of Egypt, asked him the meaning of two dreams – one in which seven fine cows were eaten by seven thin cows, and one in which seven good ears of corn were consumed by seven withered ones. Joseph said to Pharaoh:–

JOSEPH: *'God has revealed to Pharaoh what he is about to do. There will be seven years of plenty in Egypt followed by seven years of famine.'*

PHARAOH: *'Since God has shown you this, I set you over the land of Egypt.'*

STORY-TELLER: Joseph prepared grainstores in the good years. When the famine came, his brothers came from Canaan begging for corn for themselves and their father, Israel. Joseph gave them corn, saying:–

JOSEPH: *'You meant evil against me; but God meant it for good to bring it about that many people should live.'*

STORY-TELLER: Pharaoh allowed Israel and Joseph's brothers to come and live and prosper in Egypt, in Goschen. By this time, the Hebrews had begun to believe they were God's chosen people and that there was only one God, God Almighty.

[1]Canaan = The land once owned by Noah's grandson, Canaan, between Gaza and Syria.

[2]Isaac was Abraham's son by his wife, Sarah. Jacob and Esau were twin sons of Isaac and Rebecca.

[3]Really a 'long sleeved coat' worn by overseers and those who did not have to work with their hands – Joseph had, therefore, been chosen for 'management' over the heads of his brothers. This made them jealous of him.

She called his name Moses   I am the God of thy Father   Let my people go

OLD TESTAMENT SCENE 6   *The Early Life of Moses*   *c.*1320–1290 BC

(Exodus 1–11. Exodus means the 'Departure')

INTERPRETER: Through the experiences of Abraham and the Patriarchs, the Children of Israel had come to believe that God would always intervene in history to help them. We now come to the story of Moses, the greatest figure and prophet in the Old Testament. He lived in the reign of Ramses II.

STORY-TELLER: *Now there arose a new King over Egypt, who did not know Joseph.* He decided that the Hebrews were too numerous and too rich, so he made them into slaves and decreed that all male babies born to them should be killed at birth. However, one Hebrew mother hid her new-born son in a basket by the river's edge to save him. There he was found by the daughter of Pharaoh, King of Egypt, and she said:

PHARAOH'S DAUGHTER: *'This is one of the Hebrews' children. Take this child away and nurse him.'*

STORY-TELLER: She called the child Moses and brought him up as her own son. When Moses grew up and was in the desert, he saw a bush burning, and yet the bush was not consumed by the flames. As he looked, a voice called to him from the bush, saying:

VOICE OF GOD: *'I am the God of your father, the God of Abraham, the God of Isaac and the God of Jacob. I have seen the suffering of my people who are in Egypt and I have come to deliver them and to bring them to a good and broad land, a land flowing with milk and honey, to the land of Canaan. Come, I will send you to Pharaoh that you may bring my people out of Egypt.'*

STORY-TELLER: Moses asked the LORD to tell him his name, so that the people would know he had indeed talked with God:

VOICE OF GOD: *'I AM WHO I AM, Say "I AM" sent me to you.'*

INTERPRETER: 'I AM' is the literal translation of the Hebrew name for God, YAHWEH, which means 'I AM' or 'I EXIST' or even 'I AM EXISTENCE ITSELF'. This was too sacred a name for the Hebrews or for their descendants, the Jews, who came from the tribe of Israel's son, Judah, to say aloud or even to write in full. In the sixteenth century AD, a monk misspelt the word YAHWEH, writing down the word JEHOVAH instead, a name that has now entered our language.[1]

STORY-TELLER: Moses then went to Pharaoh and cried out to him:

MOSES: *'Thus says the LORD, the God of Israel, "let my people go, that they may hold a feast for me in the wilderness".'*

PHARAOH: *'I do not know the LORD, and moreover I will not let Israel go.'*

STORY-TELLER: Pharaoh refused ten times to let Israel go. Each time, the Lord sent a plague against Egypt – starting by turning the rivers to blood followed by plagues of frogs, gnats, and flies, which are depicted in the scene here. At last, after the tenth plague took the lives of all the first-born males among the Egyptians, Pharaoh then agreed to let the Children of Israel leave Egypt.

[1]In all the quotations here, LORD is spelled with capital letters. This is because the original Hebrew writers used the abbreviation YHWH in each place to avoid spelling the name of God in full, and so translators have replaced 'YHWH' with 'LORD'.

The Triumph of Moses

This day shall be unto you a Memorial   Stretch out thine hand over the sea   Thou shalt have no other God but me

OLD TESTAMENT SCENE 7

The Triumph of Moses

*c.*1290 BC

(Exodus 12–20 & Leviticus 19)

STORY-TELLER: On the eve of their departure from Egypt, Moses told the Children of Israel to eat a feast of roast lamb cooked in bitter herbs and eaten with unleavened bread. He told them this was to be the first 'Feast of Passover', a memorial to the day when the Angel of Death 'passed over' their houses when inflicting the tenth plague on the Egyptians. Moses said:

MOSES: *'Remember this day, in which you come out of Egypt. This day shall be for you a memorial day, and you shall observe it as an ordinance for ever.'*

STORY-TELLER: When the Children of Israel had marched to the shores of the Red Sea, they found out that Pharaoh had changed his mind and had sent his army to recapture them. The Lord then told Moses:

VOICE OF GOD: *'I will get glory over Pharaoh and all his host; and the Egyptians shall know that I am the LORD.'*

STORY-TELLER: As the people were terrified of being captured and taken back to Egypt, Moses spoke to them:

MOSES: *'Fear not, stand firm, and see the salvation of the LORD, which he will work for you today. The LORD will fight for you, and you only have to be still.'*

VOICE OF GOD: *'Lift up your rod, and stretch forth your hand over the sea and divide it, that the people of Israel may go on dry land through the sea.'*

STORY-TELLER: Moses stretched forth his hand over the sea, and the Lord drove the sea back by a strong east wind all night and made the sea dry land, and the waters were divided. The Children of Israel passed over to the other side safely. The Egyptians tried to follow them into the dry seabed – then the Lord told Moses to stretch forth his hand again over the sea. Immediately, the waters returned and covered the chariots and horsemen and drowned the host of Pharaoh.

Moses led the Children of Israel for two months into the desert of Sinai. When they reached Mt Sinai itself, Moses went up the mountain alone and spoke with God. It was then that God gave Moses his Ten Commandments – the Law for Israel. God also made a promise, or covenant, that, if the people obeyed his laws, they would be his chosen people. This agreement was written down, like the Ten Commandments, on tablets of stone and kept in the 'Ark of the Covenant'.

VOICE OF GOD: *'If you will obey my voice and keep my covenant, you shall be my possession among all peoples; for the earth is mine and you shall be a kingdom of priests and a holy nation.'*

INTERPRETER: The two main commandments were: *'You shall love the LORD your God with all your soul and with all your strength and Him only shall you worship; and you shall love your neighbour as yourself.'*

The full list of the Ten Commandments is given in Exodus 20 – the list is repeated in the Book of Leviticus (or 'Book of the Laws') when, in chapter 19 verse 18, Moses adds the amendment about the 'neighbours'. Some 1300 years later, Jesus of Nazareth commented: *'on these two commandments hang all the law and the prophets'.*[1]

[1] See St Matthew's gospel 22/40. These laws are the basis of the law for Jews, Christians and Muslims. In comparing these religions, we should remember that the Koran and the followers of Islam (i.e. 'submission to God') revere the first five books of the Old Testament. The Koran states (in sura – i.e. chapter – XXIII verse 38): 'We gave Moses the Book for Israel's guidance'. In sura V verse 110, the Koran also states that the 'Book' includes 'the Scripture and Wisdom and the Law AND the Gospel'. In several places, the Koran expresses Mahomet's view that both the Book and the Gospel had either been forgotten, or else distorted, by Jews and Christians. He blamed this, in the case of Christians, on the bitter controversies between the many different sects that divided the Christian communities of those days (i.e. the 6th and 7th centuries AD) on the nature of God.

The Lord used to speak to Moses face to face as a man speaks to his friend

OLD TESTAMENT SCENE 8   *Moses in the Wilderness*   *c.*1290–1250 BC

(Exodus 20–40, Numbers & Deuteronomy)

STORY-TELLER: Moses led the Children of Israel for 40 years through the wilderness of Sinai to within sight of 'the Promised Land'.[1] These wanderings are described in the second half of Exodus, Numbers and Deuteronomy.[2] The Israelites suffered many hardships and defeats. Sometimes, the people lost their faith that God would always support them. This made them turn away to other gods – but, when they repented, Moses asked the Lord to forgive them, saying:

MOSES: *'The LORD is slow to anger, and abounding in steadfast love, forgiving iniquity.'*[3]

STORY-TELLER: On these and other important occasions, Moses retired to a tent, called the 'Tent of the Meeting', to pray. The Lord concealed himself in a pillar of cloud before the tent and there he spoke *to Moses, face to face, as a man does to his friend.*[4] Sometimes, when this happened, the whole people of Israel *saw the glory of the LORD.*

On one occasion, the people were starving in the desert but the Lord fed them by sending down Manna from heaven. This fell like flakes onto the sand. After this, Moses reminded the people that:–

MOSES: *'Man does not live by bread alone, but man lives by everything that proceeds from the mouth of God.'*[5]

INTERPRETER: Nearly 1300 years later, Jesus of Nazareth was to quote these words as he rebuked the Devil for tempting him to relieve his hunger by turning a stone into bread.

STORY-TELLER: At last, when the long journey was proving too arduous and when the people were almost dying of thirst, even Moses lost heart. The Lord rebuked him for this and made him strike a rock with his staff so that fresh water gushed out to supply the people's needs. Because of this momentary loss of faith, Moses was told by God that he would not be allowed to enter the Promised Land himself – he would only see it from afar. This is what actually happened – for Moses died on the plains of Moab, overlooking Canaan. It was there that the Lord made him a promise:–

VOICE OF GOD: *'I shall raise up a prophet like you among your brethren; and I will put my words into his mouth.'*[6]

INTERPRETER: Many centuries later, Jesus referred to this, saying to his disciples: *'If you believed in Moses, you would believe in me, for he wrote of me.'*[7]

---

[1]Throughout this time, Moses was helped by his elder brother, Aaron. Since Moses had a speech impediment (see Exodus 4/10–17), Aaron used to speak his words to the people for him. Aaron died shortly before Moses.

[2]'Numbers & Deuteronomy': Numbers gets its name from a census it contains of the 12 tribes of Israel. The book is a diary of the desert wanderings. 'Deuteronomy' means 'the second giving of the Law'. It contains Moses' last commands and testament.

[3]Numbers 14/18.

[4]Exodus 33/7–11. One of the most moving descriptions of someone at prayer. Nearly 2,800 years after Moses, St Teresa of Avila gave a similar description of prayer in her autobiography: she called it 'a conversation with Him Who loves us'.

[5]Deut. 8/3.

[6]Deut. 18/18.

[7]St John's gospel 5/46. In putting *'wrote of me'*, John shows the old belief that Moses wrote all the first five books of the Old Testament – the Jewish 'Torah' – himself. See also Acts 3/22.

I will not fail thee or forsake thee

OLD TESTAMENT SCENE 9   *Moses' Successors: Joshua, the Judges,*   *c.*1250–*c.*1000 BC
King Saul

(Joshua 1–24; Judges 1–21; I Samuel 1, 2, 16; Ruth 1)

STORY-TELLER: *After the death of Moses, the servant of the LORD, the LORD said to Joshua, the son of Nun, Moses' minister:–*

VOICE OF GOD: *'Moses my servant is dead; now go over this Jordan, you and all the people, into the land which I am giving to them. As I was with Moses, so I will be with you; I will not fail you or forsake you. Be strong and of good courage'* (Joshua 1/1–6).

STORY-TELLER: Joshua then led the people over Jordan, captured Jericho and the surrounding country and, when he died of old age, the people had settled in the land. Joshua was succeeded as leader by 15 Judges over a period of 200 years. These Judges included folk-heroes like the Prophetess Deborah (who inspired Israel to defeat the army of Sisera and his 900 chariots of iron), Gideon and Samson.

Gideon is famous for storming the Midianite stronghold at night with only three hundred men, who shouted as they charged: *'For the LORD and for Gideon.'* Samson, who had been shorn of his hair by his mistress, Delilah, and was then blinded by the Philistines, crushed his enemies to death by breaking the main supporting pillars of the temple of Baal where they were worshipping. Samson died in the wreckage, having prayed to the LORD before he made his last great effort against the enemies of Israel: *'O LORD God, remember me, I pray you, and strengthen me.'*

The last Judge, the Prophet Samuel, had been called by God, after his mother Hannah had dedicated him to serve the priest Eli. Samuel had answered the Lord by saying *'Speak LORD for thy servant hears.'* Samuel ruled Israel until he grew old, when the people demanded that he should anoint a king to succeed him as their leader. Samuel was guided by the Lord to choose Saul, son of Kish, as king, and when he anointed him with sacred oil all the people shouted: *'God save the King!'*[1]

Saul proved a disappointment as king. After defeating the Amalekites, he disobeyed the Lord's command, given through Samuel, to execute the war-criminal, Agag, king of the Amalekites. The Lord therefore told Samuel to choose another to succeed Saul as king when he died, instead of Saul's sons.

Samuel chose the youngest son of Jesse, the shepherd-boy David, who was the great-grandson of Ruth and Boaz, as Saul's successor.[2]

[1] I Samuel 10/24.

[2] For the story of Ruth, one of the world's great short love-stories, see Book of Ruth. Its most famous saying, when Ruth begs her widowed mother-in-law not to send her away, is from chapter 1 verses 16 & 17:– *'Entreat me not to leave you or to return from following you; for where you go I will go, and where you lodge I will lodge; your people shall be my people, and your God my God; where you die I will die, and there will I be buried. May the LORD do so to me and more so if death parts me from you.'*

David and Goliath

OLD TESTAMENT SCENE 10   *From King Saul & King David to King Solomon and the Civil War*   *c.* 1000–925 BC

(1 Samuel 16/11 on; II Samuel 7; I Kings 1–15. See also I & II Chronicles)

STORY-TELLER: After God had guided Samuel to choose David as the future king of Israel, he anointed him and *'the Spirit of the LORD came mightily upon David from that time forwards'.*

Shortly afterwards, while Saul was still king, the Israelite army was facing the invading forces of the Philistines. David's older brothers were with Saul's army, so their father, Jesse, sent David to take them some food. When he reached the army, David found that the great Philistine champion, Goliath of Gath, had challenged the army of Israel to send out a champion of their own to fight him in single combat, and so decide which side was to be the victor. No Israelite had dared to accept the challenge.

David, who had successfully fought a lion and a bear, while guarding his father's flocks, offered to go and fight Goliath. Despite the scorn of his brothers, David was accepted by Saul, who loaded him with heavy arms and said:

KING SAUL: *'Go, and the LORD be with you!'* (I Sam. 17/37 on).

STORY-TELLER: David put on the arms *and tried in vain to go, for he was not used to them. Then David said:*

DAVID: *'I cannot go with these.'*

STORY-TELLER: *And David put them off. Then he took his staff in his hand and chose five smooth stones from the brook, and put them in his shepherd's bag; his sling was in his hand, and he drew near the Philistine. And the Philistine came on and drew near to David, with his shield-bearer in front of him. And when the Philistine looked, and saw David, he disdained him; for he was but a youth, ruddy and comely in appearance. And the Philistine said to David:*

GOLIATH: *'Am I a dog, that you come to me with sticks? Come to me and I will give your flesh to the birds.'*

DAVID: *'You come to me with a sword and with a spear and with a javelin, but I come to you in the name of the LORD of hosts, the God of the armies of Israel, whom you have defied. This day will the LORD deliver you into my hand. I will strike you down, that all may know that there is a God in Israel. And that all this assembly may know that the LORD saves not with the sword and spear; for the battle is the LORD's and he will give you into our hand.'*

STORY-TELLER: David then slung a stone at Goliath's head and struck him with such force that he fell down dead. David drew Goliath's sword and beheaded him. The armies of Israel then charged upon the Philistines, who fled away.

Soon after this, Saul became sick and jealous of David and there was civil war between them. David defeated Saul and became King of Israel.

INTERPRETER: In David's reign, the first five books of the Old Testament, the Jewish 'Torah', were put into writing. When he died, he had captured Zion, the site of Jerusalem, and had heard the Lord promise that *'your throne shall be established for ever'* (II Sam. 7/16).

David's son, Solomon, succeeded him as king and he built the Temple at Jerusalem. But, though Solomon was reputed to be wise, he was extravagant and took many foreign wives who *turned away his heart after other gods.*[1] After his death, civil wars divided Israel into two kingdoms: Israel in the north and Judah in the south.

[1] I Kings 11/4. N.B. I & II Chronicles are mainly a repeat of Kings.

Let it be known that thou art God in Israel

OLD TESTAMENT SCENE 11 *The Prophet Elijah Defeats the Prophets of Baal* c.860 BC

(I Kings 17–19 and II Kings 1 & 2)

STORY-TELLER: After the civil war, the Kingdom of Israel was based on Samaria and consisted of ten of the twelve tribes, while the tribes of Judah and Benjamin had their capital at Jerusalem. About one hundred years after the split in the tribes, Ahab, king of Israel, married Jezebel, a Phoenician, who worshipped Baal. She forced Israel to stop worshipping the Lord and to take to her god instead. So it was written that during this reign:

'King Ahab did more to provoke the LORD, the God of Israel, to anger than all the kings that went before him.'

Through Jezebel's persecution, all the prophets of the Lord except Elijah were killed. He only survived because of his fame as a miracle worker and as a prophet. He managed at last to persuade Ahab to summon the people together so that he could address them:

ELIJAH: *'How long will you go limping between two opinions? If the LORD he is God, follow him; but if Baal then follow him. I, even I only, am left a prophet of the LORD; but Baal's prophets number four hundred and fifty men.'*

STORY-TELLER: Elijah then challenged the prophets of Baal to a contest to see whose prayers would be answered by the true God and bring fire down from heaven on one of the altars that Elijah and the prophets of Baal had prepared.

The prophets of Baal accepted the challenge and prepared a sacrifice to be burned at their altar. All day long, they prayed but no fire came and Elijah mocked them, saying:

ELIJAH: *'Cry aloud, for he is a god; either he is musing, or he is on a journey, or he is asleep!'*

STORY-TELLER: Then Elijah ordered water to be poured over his sacrifice and the altar and in a ditch round the altar. He had this repeated twice over. After that, he cried out to the Lord:

ELIJAH: *'O LORD, God of Abraham, of Isaac and Israel, let it be known this day that thou art God in Israel, and that I am thy servant, and that I have done all these things at thy word.'*

STORY-TELLER: Fire then fell from heaven over Elijah's altar and consumed the sacrifice, the wood and the altar stones and all the water in the ditch. All the prophets of Baal fled and Elijah told the people to kill them all and let none escape.

After this, Queen Jezebel swore to kill Elijah. So he fled to a cave in the mountains. But the Lord caused a great wind to blow and an earthquake and then, out of the sound and fury of the elements, Elijah heard a *'still small voice'* saying *'What are you doing here, Elijah? Go, return!'*

So Elijah returned and anointed Jehu to succeed Ahab as king. As Elijah grew old, he was taken up into the sky in a chariot of fire, leaving his mantle to fall to the ground, to be taken up by his disciple, Elisha.

INTERPRETER: In this way, Elijah saved the religion of Israel and the worship of the LORD could continue.

The manner of his passing caused the Jews to believe that he would return to the earth. Nearly 900 years later, the Jews asked John the Baptist and Jesus if they were Elijah.

25

OLD TESTAMENT SCENE 12   *The Story of Israel & Judah from Elijah to Daniel*   9th–6th Cent. BC

(I Kings 19 onwards. See also II Kings and Daniel 5)

INTERPRETER: After Elijah and his disciple, Elisha, the kingdoms of Israel and Judah declined both spiritually and in power. Israel was destroyed by Assyria in 721 BC and Jerusalem was taken in 587 by Nebuchadnezzar. The remnants of Judah were exiled to Babylon. Then, after the Persians had defeated Babylon, Cyrus allowed Ezra to lead the Jews back to rebuild Jerusalem and their temple in 538 BC.

STORY-TELLER: This account is given in the books of history from Kings to Esther. The important books for this period from a spiritual point of view are those of the Prophets.[1] Sixteen of these prophets acted as the conscience of the people, the guardians of the faith and independent commentators of the political and international dangers facing the kingdoms of Israel and Judah. They did this at great risk to themselves: Daniel, shown in this scene, was thrown to the lions, Isaiah is believed by some to have been sawn in half, Jeremiah was cast alive into a pit and Jonah was swallowed by a whale.

In this scene, Daniel foretells the destruction of King Belshazzar's Babylonian Empire. The story is taken from the Book of Daniel:–

King Belshazzar and his lords, his wives and his concubines drank wine from the vessels of gold and silver which Nebuchadnezzar had taken out of the temple at Jerusalem. As they did so and praised the gods of silver and gold, bronze, iron, wood and stone, the fingers of a man's hand appeared and wrote on the plaster of the wall of the king's palace, opposite the lampstand: MENE MENE TEKEL UPHARSIN.[2]

The king saw the hand as it wrote. His colour changed, and his thoughts alarmed him; his limbs gave way, and his knees knocked together. The king cried aloud to bring in the enchanters, the Chaldaens and the astrologers and said to these wise men of Babylon:

BELSHAZZAR: *'Whoever reads this writing, and shows me its interpretation, shall be clothed in purple, and have a chain of gold about his neck, and shall be the third ruler in the kingdom.'*

STORY-TELLER: *The wise men came in, but they could not read the writing. So the Queen told Belshazzar to summon Daniel, one of the exiles of Judah, whom Nebuchadnezzar had made one of his wise men, because he was 'a man in whom is the spirit of the gods'. Daniel came in and read the words, saying:*

DANIEL: *'God has numbered the days of your kingdom and brought it to an end; you have been weighed in the balances and found wanting; your kingdom is given to the Medes and Persians.'*

STORY-TELLER: *That very night Belshazzar was slain. And Darius the Mede received the kingdom.*

INTERPRETER: Daniel was one of the great prophets whose divine revelations, received in visions sent by God, are described in the next few scenes. We will also include two stories brought back from the exile. These all show radical new ideas which changed the nature of Jewish faith and hopes.

The accounts of these visions are complicated by the way the prophets tended to telescope the present, near and far future and the 'Last Days' at the end of Time into one present action taking place before their eyes.

Isaiah, to whose visions we now turn, foretold the coming of a 'Saviour', or 'Messiah' or 'Christ' (in Greek). He also foretold some of Jesus Christ's teachings, of his death for the redemption of our sins and his final coming again in the 'Last Days', to judge the world after a general resurrection of the dead.

---

[1] The dates and mission of the prophets are given in Appendix I.
[2] From Daniel 5, 1–30.

OLD TESTAMENT SCENE 13   *The Prophet Isaiah's Visions of a Saviour, the Messiah, Christ*   8th–6th Cents. BC

(Isaiah 1–66)

(*Note*: Isaiah lived from *c*.740–690 BC. His book is the work of himself, his equally great but unknown successor and also later disciples. The book covers a period from the 8th–6th centuries BC).

(*NB: The numbers after the quotations refer to Isaiah chapters and verses unless otherwise stated.*)

INTERPRETER: Isaiah was the greatest prophet after Moses and Elijah. He began his mission to Judah by calling the people to repent:

ISAIAH: *'Come now, let us reason together, says the LORD: though your sins are like scarlet, they shall be as white as snow.'* (1/18)

STORY-TELLER: Then Isaiah prophesied what the LORD had in store for the nations of the earth.

ISAIAH: *'In the "Last Days" the house of the LORD will be established and all nations shall flow to it. He shall judge the nations and they shall beat their swords into ploughshares and their spears into pruning hooks; nation shall not lift up sword against nation, neither shall they learn war any more.'* (2/2–4)

'The sign for this shall be: A young woman shall conceive and bear a son, and shall call his name Immanuel! God is with us! Then the people who walked in darkness will have seen a great light for unto us a child is born, to us a son is given; and the government shall be upon his shoulder and his name will be called Wonderful Counsellor, Mighty God, Everlasting Father, Prince of Peace.' (7/14, 9/2 on)

STORY-TELLER: Isaiah also said that a prophet would prepare the way for this saviour who, though God's representative, would also be his beloved suffering servant:

ISAIAH: *'A voice will cry: "In the wilderness prepare the way of the LORD, make straight in the desert a highway for our God. Every valley shall be filled up and every mountain and hill will be laid low; the uneven ground shall become level and the rough places a plain. And the Glory of the LORD shall be revealed and all flesh shall see it together. For the mouth of the LORD has spoken."'* (40/3–5)

'"Behold!" says the LORD, "My servant whom I uphold; I have put my spirit upon him, he will bring justice to the nations." He will cry out: "I am LORD your Saviour and your Redeemer, and the mighty one of Jacob. The Spirit of the LORD is upon me, because the LORD has anointed me to bring good tidings to the afflicted; he has sent me to bind up the broken-hearted, to proclaim liberty to the captives, and the opening of prisons to those who are bound; to proclaim the year of the LORD's favour."' (42/1, 49/26, 61/1)

STORY-TELLER: Seven centuries later, Jesus Christ would read these words in the synagogue in Nazareth and say, as he announced his gospel, *'Today this prophecy is fulfilled in your hearing.'* (Luke 4/18)

Isaiah also foresaw that the Jews would kill their Saviour and he described how he would be:–

ISAIAH: *'. . . despised and rejected of men, a man of sorrows, and acquainted with grief, despised and we esteemed him not. Wounded for our transgressions, bruised for our iniquities, and with his stripes our wounds are healed. He was oppressed and led like a lamb to the slaughter . . . yet he bore the sin of many and made intercession for the transgressors.'* (53/3)

INTERPRETER: Isaiah's style, as this passage shows, was to telescope his visions of the near future and the far off last days into one, so that everything seems to be happening in the present. Isaiah was also the first prophet to tell that there would be a general resurrection of the dead and a day of judgement:

'The dead shall live and their bodies shall rise' . . . and *'There will be new heavens and a new earth.'* (26/19, 65/17, and Revelations 21/1)

I know that my Redeemer liveth

OLD TESTAMENT SCENE 14

The Patience and Suffering of Job
(Job 1–19)

This story is post-exile, after 538 BC

INTERPRETER: We interrupt the books of the prophets to portray the Book of Job. Like Proverbs and Ecclesiastes,[1] this is a 'Book of Wisdom'. Our purpose here is to show how the shattering experience of the exile in Babylon changed still further the Jewish ideas about God. Although the priests still showed how their sufferings were due to the sin of apostasy, the prophets began to point out how the Lord allowed the innocent to suffer undeserved pain and loss. The story of Job, brought back to Jerusalem by the exiles as they returned, illustrates this new thinking. The story begins:–

STORY-TELLER: *There was a man in the land of Uz, whose name was Job; and that man was blameless and upright, one who feared God, and turned away from evil. Now there was a day when the sons of God (that is to say, his angels), came to present themselves before the LORD, and Satan also came. The Lord asked*

VOICE OF GOD: *'Whence have you come?'*

SATAN: *'From going to and fro on the earth, and from walking up and down it.'*

VOICE OF GOD: *'Have you considered my servant Job, that there is none like him on the earth, a blameless and upright man, who fears God and turns away from evil?'*

SATAN: *'Does Job fear God for nought? Hast thou not put a hedge about him and his house and all that he has, on every side? Thou has blessed the work of his hands, and his possessions have increased in the land. But put forth thy hand, and touch all that he has, and he will curse thee to thy face!'*

VOICE OF GOD: *'Behold, all that he has is in your power; only upon himself do not put your hand.'*

STORY-TELLER: Satan then destroyed one by one all Job's flocks, his house, his servants, his children and ruined him, leaving him covered in sores, scraping his skin with a potsherd, seated on a dunghill. Job says:–

JOB: *'Naked I came from my mother's womb and naked I shall return; the LORD gave and the LORD has taken away; Blessed be the name of the LORD.'*

STORY-TELLER: *In all this Job did not sin or charge God with wrong: Job's wife then told him:*

JOB'S WIFE: *'Do you still hold fast to your integrity? Curse God and die!'*

JOB: *'You speak as one of the foolish women would speak. Shall we receive good at the hand of God, and shall we not receive evil?'*

STORY-TELLER: Three friends of Job, Eliphaz, Bildad and Zophar, then came to comfort Job. Condescendingly, they tried to convince him, with their old-fashioned beliefs, that Job must have sinned greatly to have been made to suffer so much. Job swore that he had committed no sin. After prolonged discussions, Job burst out at them saying:

JOB: *'Miserable Comforters are you all! I also could speak as you do, if you were in my place! BUT I KNOW THAT MY REDEEMER LIVES, and at last I shall stand upon earth, then from my flesh shall I see God, whom I shall see on my side.'[2]*

[1]These two books, like the 'Song of Solomon', should be read for their own sakes. They do not fit into the main Bible story as presented here. They contain some famous maxims e.g. *'Wisdom is better than rubies'* (Prov. 8/11) and *'a good name is better than precious ointment'* (Ecc. 7/1) and *'cast thy bread upon the waters'* (Ecc. 11/1); also some fine writing . . . e.g. the famous passage from Ecc. 12/1 on. Their message, like that of Psalm 111/10, is that 'All is vanity . . . but fear of the Lord is the beginning of wisdom.'

[2]Job 19/25. 'Redeemer' here probably means 'Vindicator', whose role was to see justice done for a kinsman; i.e. an umpire – probably not yet the Jewish 'Messiah' though Christians have traditionally taken this to be Job's meaning. See also penultimate paragraph on prayer, page 113 below.

OLD TESTAMENT SCENE 15   *Job Weakens, but at Last Sees God*   Post-exile, after 538 BC

(Job 20–42)

STORY-TELLER: Job's friends still would not leave him alone. Job cursed the day he was born and, at last, accused God of warring against him and being unfair to him by not letting him plead his case:

JOB: *'I cry to thee and thou dost not answer me. Thou hast turned cruel to me; thou dost persecute me!'*

STORY-TELLER: At this outburst, Job's three friends gave up, seeing that he was *'righteous in his own eyes'*. A fourth younger friend, Elihu, now joined in and reproved Job:–

ELIHU: *'The Almighty will not pervert justice. Job speaks without knowledge, his words are without insight. He adds rebellion to his sin.'*

STORY-TELLER: Elihu then explained that mortals cannot understand fully the ways of God:

ELIHU: *'God thunders wondrously with his voice; he does great things which we cannot comprehend. God speaks in one way, and in two, though man does not perceive.'*

STORY-TELLER: *Then the LORD answered Job out of the whirlwind:*

VOICE OF GOD: *'Who is this that darkens counsel by words without knowledge? Gird up your loins like a man, I will question you. Where were you when I laid foundations of the earth? Tell me if you have the understanding. Who determined its measurements – surely you know?'*

STORY-TELLER: God then poured out question after question at Job, showing how the world he created and the mind of God were quite beyond Job's powers to understand.

VOICE OF GOD: *'Have you commanded the morning since your days began and caused the dawn to know its place?*

'Have you entered the springs of the sea? Have the gates of death been revealed to you? Do you give the horse his might? Is it by your wishes that the hawk soars and spreads wings toward the south? Tell me, shall a fault finder contend with the Almighty? He who argues with God must answer! Will you condemn me that you may be justified?'

STORY-TELLER: At last, Job realised that God was infinitely greater than he had imagined or learned from the traditional Judaic theology. Job submitted to God, confessing his ignorance and limited powers of understanding.

JOB: *'I have uttered what I do not understand, things too wonderful for me, which I do not know, I had heard of thee by the hearing of an ear, but now my eye sees thee; therefore I despise myself, and repent in dust and ashes.'*

INTERPRETER: The Lord forgave Job, chastised his friends for their limited vision and restored Job to his former status. Thus Job's original belief in a fair trial was justified. However, if we ignore the artificial start, we see that the story portrays the world we know, in which natural and man-made tragedies occur unchecked by divine intervention. God implied to Job that this is because his creation is what it is; if he were to intervene, except by giving us faith and strength to cope, he would have to change everything, performing endless miracles. There would be little point in mankind's existence in such a miracle world. Job's problem was made worse because he had no assurance of a future life. Only with Christ's death for our sins and his resurrection would it be possible to know that God loves us and that we can have faith and hope for the future.

Salvation is of the Lord

OLD TESTAMENT SCENE 16

Jonah and the Whale

(Jonah 1–4)

Another story brought
back from the exile

INTERPRETER: The story of Jonah is important to Christians as Jesus mentioned it twice.[1] It shows that not only should we obey God but also that he can save us if we have faith. Finally, it is a new concept for the Jews, since it emphasises that their religion should be taught to Gentiles (i.e. pagans).

STORY-TELLER: The story of Jonah is the only more or less humorous book in the Bible. It presents the hero as a caricature of an old-fashioned prophet who does not believe in those new-fangled ideas, even if they do come from the Lord.

In the picture, Jonah can be seen as he is about to be swallowed by a whale. Before this, he had been told by God to preach the word of God to Israel's ancient enemy, the people of Nineveh. Jonah fled, took ship from Joppa, to avoid obeying – and to flee from – the Lord. God sent a storm that threatened to sink the ship. Jonah then admitted to the crew that he was the culprit whom the Lord sought to destroy. He was thrown overboard and was swallowed by a whale, sent by God for this very purpose.

Jonah spent three days and three nights in the whale. He prayed to God and promised to fulfil God's commands, saying:

JONAH: *'Salvation is of the Lord.'*[2]

STORY-TELLER: Jonah was thrown on to dry land by the whale and went to Nineveh, where he preached to such good effect that all the population was converted to the worship of the Lord. Their sins were therefore forgiven.

Jonah, however, was disgusted at the result, for he had no time for pagans. So he went and sulked on a hill overlooking the city. The Lord then played a trick on Jonah to teach him a lesson. He made a great gourd grow up in the night to give Jonah shade from the sun. Jonah was pleased, but then the Lord made a worm eat and wither the gourd. At this, Jonah was angry and was so over-powered by the heat of the sun that he said:

JONAH: *'It is better for me to die than to live.'*

STORY-TELLER: *But God said to Jonah:*

GOD: *'Do you do well to be angry for the plant?'*

JONAH: *'I do well to be angry, angry enough to die!'*

GOD: *'You pity the plant for which you did not labour, and should not I pity Nineveh, that great city, in which there are more than a hundred and twenty-thousand persons who do not know their right hand from their left, and also much cattle?'*[3]

---

[1]See St Matthew 12/40 and 16/4; (also Luke 11/30) *'For as Jonah became a sign to the men of Nineveh, so will the Son of Man be to this generation.'* Jesus also likened Jonah's three days and nights in the whale to his own forthcoming burial in the tomb.
[2]Salvation = Forgiveness.
[3]The prophet Jonah is not the same as the Jonah referred to in II Kings 14/25, who lived in the reign of King Jeraboam *c.*930 BC. The prophet Jonah's mission to Nineveh was possibly in about 760 BC.

I shall pour out my Spirit upon all flesh

I shall raise unto David a righteous branch   *Jeremiah*

I saw in the night's vision one like the Son of Man   *Daniel*

Thou Bethlehem...out of thee shall he come forth   *Micah*

OLD TESTAMENT SCENE 17   *More Visions of the Messiah and of the Last Days*   8th to 5th Cent. BC

(From Nine Books of the Prophets)

INTERPRETER: The nine prophets, besides Isaiah, who also contributed greatly to the idea that a Messiah, or Christ, would come to save the Jewish people were Jeremiah, Ezekiel, Joel, Daniel, Amos, Micah, Zechariah and Malachi and Hosea.* Four of them are depicted in this illustration. Between them, they foretold not only that the Saviour would come, but also the place where he would be born and the way he would ride in triumph into Jerusalem.

STORY-TELLER: The Prophet Jeremiah, who also wrote 'Lamentations', is here holding the family tree of the Royal House of David as he prophesies the coming of the Messiah, a king and saviour:–

JEREMIAH: *'I will raise unto David a righteous branch and in his days Judah shall be saved.'*[1]

'I will then make a new Covenant with the House of Judah. I will put my law within them, and I will write it upon their hearts; and I will be their God, and they shall be my people. I will forgive their iniquity, and I will remember their sin no more.'[2]

STORY-TELLER: The Prophet Daniel, shown here with the lion from whose den he escaped safely, had visions of the 'Last Days', to which Jesus was to refer in Jerusalem before his crucifixion:

DANIEL: *'I saw in the night visions, and behold, with the clouds of heaven there came one like a son of man, and to him was given glory and kingdom, that all peoples, nations, and languages should serve him. His dominion is an everlasting kingdom which shall not pass away.'*[3]

Before this, however, *'there shall be a time of trouble, such as never has been.'*

'At that time shall arise Michael, the great prince who has charge over your people[4] *and many of those who sleep in the dust of the earth shall awake, some to everlasting life, and some to shame and everlasting contempt.'*[5]

STORY-TELLER: Joel, who prophesied after the exile, proclaimed that in the Last Days:–

JOEL: *'The LORD says "I will pour out my Spirit on all flesh; your sons and daughters shall prophesy, your old men shall dream dreams, and your young men shall see visions."'*[6]

INTERPRETER: St Peter the Apostle would remind the people of this in his speech at Pentecost after the Holy Spirit had descended on the heads of the Apostles gathered in Jerusalem.[7] St Peter's words were: *'This is what was spoken by the Prophet Joel.'*

STORY-TELLER: The fourth prophet Micah in our picture can be seen pointing to a city on a hill and saying:

MICAH: *'You, O Bethlehem Ephratah, who are little among the clans of Judah, from you shall come forth to me one who is to be ruler in Israel, whose origin is from of old, from the ancient of days.'*[8]

STORY-TELLER: The prophets Ezekiel, Zechariah and Malachi between them foretold the dead would arise at Day of Judgement, that the Messiah would enter Jerusalem riding on an ass and that, before the *'great and terrible day of the LORD'*, the prophet Elijah would return to earth.[9]

---

*See Hosea 6/2 for earliest prophecy of Christ's resurrection on the third day.
[1] Jer. 23/5.
[2] Jer. 31/32–4.
[3] Dan. 7/13–15.
[4] Archangel Michael.
[5] Dan. 12/1–4.
[6] Joel 2/28.
[7] Acts 2/14 on.
[8] Micah 5/2.
[9] Ezek. 37/12. Zech 9/9. Malachi 4/5 – Malachi is the last book in the Old Testament written about 450 BC.

Let everything that breathes praise the Lord

OLD TESTAMENT SCENE 18

The Psalms of David

(Psalms 1–150)

11th–3rd Cent. BC

INTERPRETER: We have left the Book of Psalms until last because it is entirely different from the rest – being a set of 150 'Songs of Praise'. These were used for ceremonial and liturgical purposes. They were written first in the reign of King David. They were often revised and brought up to date by adding new themes. The final version seems to have been about 3rd century BC. One of the latest psalms to have been written – designed to bring in the new religious thinking after the Exile – was the 'Messianic Psalm', no. 96. This refers to the Messiah, Christ who *'will judge the world with righteousness'*. Psalm 2 verse 5 also refers to the future Christ: *'You are my Son. Today I have begotten you . . . blessed are they who take refuge in him.'*[1]

The Psalms are sung with equal fervour today in synagogues, churches and chapels and, together with the writings in the Apocrypha, they help to form a bridge between the Old and New Testaments. Our Lord referred to them on a number of occasions and even quoted words from two of them, almost with his last breath, as he hung dying on the Cross:

STORY-TELLER: The two psalms he quoted were psalms 22 and 31. The words from these that are recorded by St Matthew and St Mark:[2] *'My God, My God, why hast thou forsaken me?'* seem to suggest that Jesus was in a state of utter despair but, if we read further in Psalm 22, we find that, far from being in despair, our Lord was trying to tell his disciples of the exciting prospect ahead as they spread his gospel. Among these words is the prophesy that *'Men shall tell of the LORD to coming generations and proclaim his deliverance to a people yet unborn!'*

Similarly, St Luke quotes Psalm 31 as Jesus' dying words: *'Into thy hands I commit my Spirit . . .'*[3] If we read further, we find that our Lord was striving to give words of great encouragement :–

'Love the LORD, all his saints! The LORD preserves the faithful. Be strong, and let your heart take courage, all you who wait for the LORD!'

Thus, even as his human life-blood ebbed away, his spirit strove to speak on through his broken frame. Never in all his life on Earth was there a better example of our Lord's dual nature, wholly divine and wholly human.

INTERPRETER: The Psalms were extremely important to our Lord and, after his Resurrection shortly before he ascended into heaven, St Luke's gospel records that he reminded his disciples of all he had told them, ending with these words: *'These are my words which I spoke to you, while I was still with you, that everything written about me in the law of Moses and the Prophets AND THE PSALMS must be fulfilled.'*[4]

STORY-TELLER: Let us now end these old testament scenes with this rousing Psalm 150:– *'PRAISE THE LORD! Praise God in his sanctuary: Praise him in his mighty firmament! Praise him for his mighty deeds, praise him according to his greatness! Praise him with the trumpet and sound, praise him with the lute and harp! Praise him with the timbrel and dance; praise him with strings and pipe! Praise him with sounding cymbals! Let everything that has breath praise the LORD! PRAISE THE LORD!*

[1]See also Hebrews 1/5.
[2]Matt 27/46; Mark 15/34 and Psalm 22/1. See also Crucifixion page 93 below.
[3]Luke 23/46 and Psalm 31/5.
[4]St Luke chapter 24/44.

SCENE FROM THE APOCRYPHA *The Apocrypha or 'Hidden Books'* 2nd Cent. BC to 1st Cent. AD

(The Book of Tobit and others)

INTERPRETER: In the centuries after the writing of the last books of the Old Testament and the re-writing and editing of the books destroyed during the Babylonian exile, a collection of books was produced over a period of about two hundred and fifty years. They are not in the Old Testament Canon, but are regarded as 'worth reading' by both Jews and Christians. These books were set aside by the Jews and called the 'Hidden Books' or the Apocryphal books.

A story from one of these is illustrated opposite: the story of Tobias and the Angel from the Apocryphal Book of Tobit.

STORY-TELLER: The boy Tobias, son of Tobit, is shown with his dog and the Archangel Raphael, one of the seven messengers of God, according to the Jews. Tobias has just caught a fish in the River Tigris having been sent on a mission to Persia by his blind father, Tobit. The angel shows Tobias how to cure his father's blindness using the fish's liver.

The one famous saying in this story is that: *'Whatever you hate, do to no man.'* This is a negative form of the 'Golden Rule' quoted by Jesus in his Sermon on the Mount that:

'Whatever you wish men to do to you, do so to them. This is the Law and the Prophets.'[1]

INTERPRETER: The importance of the Apocrypha is that many of the books help to give us a picture of life in Palestine and of the attitudes of priests and religious sects at the time of Our Lord's birth. Esdras, for instance, helps us to understand the thinking of Judaism after the reforms brought about by the puritan influence of the Pharisees.

The Pharisees believed in the prospect of a general resurrection of the dead, in which the priestly caste of the Sadducees did not believe. By the time Jesus was born, the Pharisees had ceased to be a good influence. They had degenerated into believing that they would be 'right with God' at the Day of Judgement, provided they had kept a perfect outward show of formal obedience to the Law and observed a number of ostentatious religious practices. They had also become the drill-sergeants or martinets of Judaism, and so were bound to come into conflict with Our Lord's more liberal approach to religion. He wanted to revive and deepen the spiritual approach to the meaning and practice of the Law, which they had neglected, as he would tell them in no uncertain terms in Jerusalem:

'you tithe mint and cummin, and have neglected the weightier matters of the Law, justice, and mercy and faith'.[2]

Finally, these writings of the Apocrypha also show that there was a positive fever of expectation and speculative debate about the signs that would indicate the 'coming of the Kingdom'. This is why Jesus and John the Baptist only had to say *'The Kingdom of Heaven is at hand'* to find crowds surging round them to hear *'the good news'*.

[1]Matthew 7/12.
[2]Matthew 23/23.

The New Creation

'In the Beginning was the Word, and the Word was with God, and the Word was God . . . and the Word Became Flesh and Dwelt Among Us.'

NEW TESTAMENT SCENE 1   *St John's Prologue to His Gospel:* 'In the Beginning was the Word'[1]   John I

STORY-TELLER: The New Testament – or New Covenant – marks a new beginning. The Old Testament records various 'covenants' or treaties between God and humankind and a long history of encounters with God through visions and other religious or spiritual experiences. The New Testament gives the story and interpretations of how God at last came down to earth in the person of Jesus of Nazareth – in other words, how God became man – made flesh – God Incarnate. St Paul described this and God's purpose as: *'When the time had come, God sent forth his Son, born of woman under the law, to redeem those under the law, so that they might be adopted as sons!'*[2]

St John – whose prologue to his gospel we illustrate here – gives the intellectual or philosophical interpretation of this event. In these first 18 verses – the usual gospel reading for Christmas Day, the birthday of Jesus – he explains Jesus' origin and nature and the significance of his coming and of his teaching. This prologue is packed with symbolic meaning.

INTERPRETER: The words round the picture are taken from these first 18 verses of St John's gospel. St John uses 'The Word' to mean Jesus:–

In the beginning was the Word, and the Word was with God and the Word was God. He was in the beginning with God; all things were made through him, and without him was not anything made that was made. In him was life and the light of men. The light shines in the darkness, and the darkness has not overcome it. . . . And the Word became flesh and dwelt among us, full of grace and truth.

The 'Word', or Logos in Greek, is Jesus. He was there at the beginning of creation as part of God – the agent of creation.[3] It was through him that God became flesh to bring light to us out of darkness.

STORY-TELLER: We show this taking place in the picture – as the hands of God create Jesus by introducing his own Holy Spirit into a human cell – thus becoming 'flesh'. God's Spirit is indicated by the small filament of light burning red with the letters 'YHWH'. This is the Jewish symbol for the name of God.

This symbol, sometimes called the 'Word' by the Jews, was used by them for 'YAHWEH', the name for God which was too sacred for them to write down or to say aloud in full. The Jews in John's audience would therefore have understood that he meant God and Jesus were one – that Jesus was God made flesh. The Greeks among his readers would also have understood what he meant – for to them the 'Word', Logos, was the name given to the 'Mind of God' by their own philosophers in the fifth century BC.[4]

INTERPRETER: These first 18 verses have been called the greatest literary pearl among the gospel writings. They are filled with allusions to the Old Testament – *In the beginning . . .*', for example, reminds us of the opening words of Genesis – thus implying the idea of a 'New Creation'. This is underlined by the reference to 'light' – for God said *'Let there be light'*, as he created the universe. By *'life and light'*, St John also reminds us of Isaiah's prophecy of a *'light to them that sit in darkness'* – when the Saviour comes.

STORY-TELLER: Also included in this passage from the gospel is St John's description of how Jesus was rejected by the people to whom he was sent. This is followed by his assertion that *to all who received him, who believed in his name, he gave power to become children of God.* After this, John shows the significance of Jesus' message compared with the message of the Old Testament – *the Law was given by Moses; grace and truth came through Jesus Christ.*[5] Finally, John says that now, once again, Jesus *'the only Son – is in the bosom of the Father'.* St John shows in this prologue that God, Jesus and the Spirit are one – three persons in one God – the Holy Trinity.

[1]For dates and authorship of the gospels see Appendix II. [2]Galatians 4/4. [3]See also John 8/58 and Col. 1/15–20. See also p. 75 below. [4]The connection between ancient Greek philosophy and Christianity is made obvious in early Byzantine Icons (Icon = Image) and in the plan of the groups of Icons (or iconostatis) before the altars of Greek and Russian Orthodox churches. It helps to explain why the Greeks were converted so easily by St Paul. See 'Icons' (the mystical origins of Christianity) by Richard Temple (Element Books, 1990). [5]Grace = forgiveness.

NEW TESTAMENT SCENE 2   *The Annunciation to the Virgin Mary &*
the Birth of John the Baptist

St Luke 1 and St Matthew 1)

STORY-TELLER: In contrast to St John's theoretical or theological approach in the prologue to his gospel, we now come to the historical versions given in the gospels of St Luke and St Matthew. According to St Luke:–

In the days of Herod, King of Judaea, there was a priest named Zecharaiah. He had a wife called Elizabeth. And they were righteous before God. While he was serving as a priest in the temple there appeared to him an angel of the Lord, Zecharaiah was troubled when he saw him. But the angel – who was Gabriel – *said to him:–*

GABRIEL: *'Do not be afraid Zecharaiah. Your prayer is heard and your wife Elizabeth will bear you a son and you shall name him John. He will be filled with the Holy Spirit and he will turn many of the sons of Israel to the Lord their God. He will go before him in the spirit of Elijah to make a people prepared.'*

STORY-TELLER: Elizabeth conceived a child. Then, six months later, the archangel Gabriel appeared to Elizabeth's cousin, Mary – who was engaged to marry Joseph. Gabriel said to her:–

GABRIEL: *'Hail Mary . . . Blessed are you among women, the Lord is with you. You will bear a son and call his name Jesus.*[1] *He shall be called the Son of the Most High; and the Lord will give him the throne of his father David, and he shall reign over the house of Jacob; and of his kingdom there shall be no end.*

MARY: *'How shall this be since I have no husband?'*

GABRIEL: *'The Holy Spirit will come upon you, therefore the child shall be called Holy, the Son of God.'*[2]

STORY-TELLER: Mary at once went to visit her cousin Elizabeth to tell her this news. She also sang to her the hymn we now call the 'Magnificat':– *'My soul magnifies the lord . . . for he has regarded the low estate of his handmaiden.'*

At about this same time – according to St Matthew's gospel – Gabriel also appeared to Joseph, to tell him that Mary was with child by the Holy Spirit. At first, Joseph was shocked – then he submitted to God's will and agreed to marry Mary. Three months later – when Elizabeth's son was born – the future 'John the Baptist' – they took him to see Zecharaiah in the Temple. He took John in his arms and sang the hymn we call the 'Benedictus':–

ZECHARIAH: *'Blessed be the Lord God of Israel for he has visited and redeemed his people. Your child will be called the prophet of the Most High . . . you will go before the face of the Lord to prepare his ways.'*

INTERPRETER: The Virginal Conception of Mary – described only in these two gospels – has been regarded as a divine mystery since the earliest days of the Church. These accounts – and the ones of Jesus' birth described in the next set of pictures – seem to be based on an oral tradition that preceded the actual writing of the gospels. There was also a tradition that St Luke's source for his story may have been Mary herself – and that St Matthew's source may have been Joseph or else a member of Joseph's family.

St Luke claims in his gospel that he obtained his information from eye-witnesses. This suggests personal knowledge of Mary, whom he could have visited at Ephesus in her retirement there with St John – Luke only lived 200 miles away in Bythinia. His statement in the gospel – which we shall read in the next scene – that *Mary kept all these things in her heart* – certainly supports the view that he had met her, perhaps in her old age.

[1]Jesus means 'He shall save'.
[2]The Virginal Conception: It is interesting to compare Luke's and Matthew's accounts with Mahomet's in the Koran. Mahomet seems to have believed in this miracle by the Holy Spirit of God. In the Koran, sura XXI and LXVI read: *'Mary, into whose womb we breathed our spirit'*. But in sura XIX we find Jesus is made to claim – at his birth – to be only a prophet and not Son of God – a non-sequitur in this context.

The Adoration of the Shepherds and Wise Men

I bring you Tidings of Great Joy

You will find the babe wrapped in swaddling clothes & lain in a manger

We have seen His Star in the east and we have come to worship Him

NEW TESTAMENT SCENE 3   *The Birth of Jesus and Adoration of the Shepherds and Wise Men*

(St Luke 2 and St Matthew 2)

STORY-TELLER: The birth stories of Jesus anchor him down in history as having been born into our world as proper flesh and blood, not just an intangible idea. According to St Luke, nine months after Gabriel visited Mary, she was taken by Joseph to Bethlehem, the city of his forefather, David. *While they were there, the time came for her to be delivered. She gave birth to her first-born child and wrapped him in swaddling cloths, and laid him in a manger because there was no room at the inn. There were shepherds out in the field, watching their flock by night. The angel of the Lord appeared to them, and the glory of the Lord shone round them. The angel said:*

ANGEL: *'Be not afraid; for I bring you news of great joy; for to you is born this day in the city of David a Saviour, who is Christ the Lord. You will find the babe lying in a manger.'*

STORY-TELLER: *The shepherds went in haste and found Mary and Joseph and the babe. And when they saw it they made known what the angel had told them. And Mary kept all these things in her heart.*

St Matthew now takes over the story from St Luke. He tells how wise men came from the East to worship Jesus as 'King of the Jews'. They had seen his star and had followed it all the way *till it came to rest over the place where the child was*. They brought gifts of gold, frankincense and myrrh. The meaning of these gifts can be seen in the lines of this hymn: *'Solemn gifts of mystic meaning, Incense doth a God disclose, Gold a royal child proclaimeth, Myrrh a future tomb foreshows.'*[1]

St Matthew ends his birth story by telling us that both Joseph and the wise men were warned in dreams that Herod the Great[2] was plotting to kill Jesus. So Joseph took Jesus and Mary away to safety.

INTERPRETER: The birth stories of Luke and Matthew are not mentioned elsewhere in the New Testament. The other two gospels and the Letters emphasise the evidence of the Resurrection as the ultimate ground for faith that Jesus was the Son of God – God Incarnate. This staggering miracle nevertheless implies that there must have been an equally great miracle at Jesus' conception. The special point which the birth stories emphasise is the nature of Jesus himself – at once wholly divine, through the activity of the Holy Spirit, and also wholly human through the willing co-operation of the Virgin Mary.

Some Christian scholars, who believe in the miracle of the Incarnation – that Jesus was God made flesh – nevertheless question whether these birth stories are real history. They suggest they are imagery symbolic of a divine truth. This does not do justice to the element of mystery which surrounds all the great acts of God – ever since the first creation.

There are some things which cannot be explained. In fact, if one considers the nature of what must have happened to Mary and Joseph, these stories seem all the more believable. This is because, compared with even the least spiritual experiences – in themselves hard to recall or to evaluate – their experiences would have been overwhelming. In such circumstances, they could hardly be expected to have realled everything that happened to them. This preserves the mystery and leaves open the question as to how precisely God achieved his purpose through the action of his Spirit.

STORY-TELLER: We take the traditional view over this divine mystery – though the matter is one of faith. However, all who believe in the Incarnation – and in the other evidence in the New Testament, that Jesus was all he ever claimed to be – *'I and the Father are one'*, *'I am in the Father and the Father in me'*[3] – can accept as true that the Holy Spirit was involved at Jesus' conception. All who believe this can say – with the traditionalists – that Jesus *'was conceived by the Holy Ghost, born of the Virgin Mary'* – as in the words of the Apostles Creed.

[1] New English Hymns 48.
[2] Herod the Great died in 4 BC. Thus Jesus must have been born about 4–6 BC. The official start of the Christian Era was miscalculated by a monk in the Middle Ages.
[3] See John 10/30 and John 14/11.

A light to lighten the Gentiles · I must be about my Father's business · My Beloved Son, in you I am well pleased

NEW TESTAMENT SCENE 4   *The Early Life of Jesus of Nazareth*

(Luke 2 and Mark 1)

STORY-TELLER: These three scenes cover the early life of Jesus until his baptism at the age of thirty. The first picture shows Joseph and Mary presenting Jesus in the Temple to the old man Simeon and to the prophetess Anna, for the ceremony of 'Purification'. This ceremony, known as 'Epiphany' in Christian churches, is one of the three principal festival days, the others being Easter and Pentecost. Epiphany is celebrated on January 6th each year.[1] Simeon had been told by the Holy Spirit that *'he would not see death until he has seen the Lord's Christ'*. As he saw Jesus, the Spirit moved him to recognise him at once as the future Saviour and he took him in his arms and sang the hymn we call the 'Nunc Dimittis':

SIMEON: *'LORD now lettest thou thy servant depart in peace according to thy word; for my eyes have seen thy salvation which thou hast prepared in the presence of all peoples, a light for revelation to gentiles and to thy people in Jerusalem.'*

STORY-TELLER: Anna then took him in her arms and gave thanks and spoke of him to all those who were looking *'for the redemption of Jerusalem'*.

In the second scene, twelve years later, Joseph and Mary had again brought Jesus to the Temple in Jerusalem. On the way home, they and their party had found Jesus was missing. So they returned to the Temple and found Jesus discussing the Scriptures in a learned way with the teachers. Mary said:–

MARY: *'Son, why have you treated us thus? Behold your father and I have been looking for you anxiously.'*

JESUS: *'How is it that you sought me? Did you not know that I must be about my Father's business?'*

STORY-TELLER: *'Mary kept all these things in her heart.'* Jesus then returned to Nazareth and *'increased in wisdom and in stature and in favour with God and man'*.

Eighteen years later, when he was thirty, Jesus went to be baptized by John the Baptist, who had been preaching the 'coming of the Kingdom' and baptizing in the river Jordan all who repented. John had told the people:

JOHN: *'As it is written in the Book of Isaiah: "The voice of one crying in the wilderness: Prepare the way for the Lord, make his paths straight . . ."*

'I baptize you with water; but he who is mightier than I is coming, the thong of whose sandals I am not worthy to untie; he will baptize you with the Holy Spirit and with fire.'

INTERPRETER: John the Baptist is therefore cast in the role of Elijah, the forerunner, prophesied by Isaiah and by the prophet Malachi. As we shall see, John's own faith in Jesus was to come later, when he sent his disciples to ask Jesus *'are you he who is to come?'* In the meantime, although Simeon and Anna, two well-known holy people, had recognised Jesus instantly, John continued his own mission as the forerunner of the promised Saviour, the Messiah. While he did so, Jesus came to meet him by the River Jordan to be baptized:–

STORY-TELLER: *When all the people were baptized, and Jesus also had been baptized and was praying, the heaven opened, and the Holy Spirit descended upon him in bodily form, as a dove, and a voice came from heaven . . .*

VOICE FROM HEAVEN: *'Thou art my beloved Son; with thee I am well pleased.'*

[1]The Feast of Epiphany is the peak of the Church's celebrations in Advent, not Christmas Day itself. A fourth feast, the Transfiguration, is of major importance in the Orthodox Church – but it is also honoured by the Anglican and Roman Catholic Churches – on August 6th, though the Orthodox date for this varies.

Begone, Satan!

The Spirit of the Lord is upon me.

Come follow me and I will make you Fishers of Men

NEW TESTAMENT SCENE 5   *Jesus' Temptations: He Announces His Ministry: He Chooses His First Disciples*

(Matthew 4 & Luke 4. See also Mark 1)

INTERPRETER: In the first picture, Jesus is shown being tempted by Satan. The story, given in detail only by Matthew and Luke, shows how Jesus – conscious of his destiny to win the world for God – was tempted to do so in the same ways that men usually do who want to conquer:– first to get the good things of life, second, to gain military conquest of all the kingdoms of the world; third, to win by displaying his supernatural gifts. He rejects them all as unworthy. Instead, he takes the hard way – as in the second picture – determined to preach the gospel of the love of God, of repentance and faith. To help him do this, he chooses – in the third scene – the sort of men as his disciples, who will do the job.

STORY-TELLER: *Jesus, full of the Holy Spirit, returned from Jordan and was led by the Spirit for 40 days in the wilderness, tempted by the devil. And he ate nothing in those days; and he was hungry. The devil said to him:*

SATAN: *'If you are the Son of God, command this stone to become bread.'*

JESUS: *'It is written, "Man shall not live by bread alone."'*[1]

STORY-TELLER: Satan tempted him twice more. He answered: *'You shall worship the Lord your God and him only'*[2] and *'You shall not tempt the Lord your God.' 'Begone Satan!'* Each time he quoted Moses.[3]

Satan then left him and Jesus went to preach in Galilee, saying:–

JESUS: *'The time is fulfilled, and the kingdom of heaven is at hand, repent and believe in the gospel.'*

STORY-TELLER: St Luke then describes in the second scene how Jesus transferred his teaching to Nazareth. Here in his own synagogue, he read from the Book of Isaiah, chapter 61, the prophesies concerning himself:

JESUS: *'The Spirit of the Lord is upon me, because he has appointed me to preach the good news to the poor. He has sent me to proclaim the release of the captives and recovering sight to the blind . . . and to proclaim the acceptable year of the LORD. Today this scripture is fulfilled in your hearing!'*[4]

STORY-TELLER: These words amounted to a claim by Jesus that he was the Messiah. The congregation got angry and said he had blasphemed. Jesus replied:

JESUS: *'No prophet is acceptable in his own country.'*

STORY-TELLER: The congregation set upon Jesus, dragged him to a hilltop to kill him, but *'. . . he passing through them went his way'*. He walked to Lake Galilee and summoned four fishermen to join him as his first disciples. They were Simon Peter, his brother Andrew, and James and John, the sons of Zebedee. Jesus said to them:–

JESUS: *'Come follow me and I will make you fishers of men!'*

STORY-TELLER: The four fishermen forsook their nets and followed Jesus. It was here that, according to St Luke, Jesus enabled Simon Peter and his crew to make a miraculous catch of fish. Peter then fell down on his knees and called Jesus 'Lord'. This part of the story is also told by St John, but only at the end of his gospel, as the last incident in Jesus' appearances after his resurrection.

[1]Deuteronomy 8/3.
[2]Deut 6/13.
[3]Deut 6/16. Also refer to page 19, Moses in the Wilderness.
[4]Luke 4/16–21.

51

You have kept the good wine until now

NEW TESTAMENT SCENE 6   # The Miracle at the Wedding in Cana

(St John 2)

STORY-TELLER: *There was a marriage at Cana in Galilee, and the mother of Jesus was there; Jesus also was invited to the marriage with his disciples. When the wine gave out, the mother of Jesus said to him:*

MARY: *'They have no wine.'*

JESUS: *'O woman, what have you to do with me? My hour is not yet come.'*

STORY-TELLER: *His mother said to the servants:*

MARY: *'Do whatever he tells you.'*

JESUS: *'Fill the jars with water.'*

STORY-TELLER: *And they filled them to the brim.*

JESUS: *'Now draw out, and take it to the steward of the feast.'*

STORY-TELLER: *When the steward of the feast tasted the water now became wine, and did not know where it had come from (though the servants who had drawn the water knew), he called the bridegroom and said:*

STEWARD: *'Every man serves the good wine first; and when men have drunk freely, then the poor wine; but you have kept the good wine until now.'*

INTERPRETER: St John probably recorded this story to show that Jesus was the Messiah bringing the good news – something much better than Judaism. The 'New Wine' is the new gospel. By using the stone water vessels used for purification of the Jews at ceremonies like this, Jesus implied that his gospel was meant to refresh the old-style religious practices of the Jews and give them greater vigour and meaning.

St Mark sums up this idea in a similar way: *'No one puts new wine into old wineskins; if he does, the wine will burst the skins, and the wine is lost and so are the skins; but new wine is for fresh skins'.* (Mk. 2/21 & 22).

Arise take up your bed and walk

NEW TESTAMENT SCENE 6 — *The Healing of the Paralysed Man*

(St Mark 2. See also Luke 5/17–27 & Matthew 9/2–8)

STORY-TELLER: All three synoptic gospels[1] include this story of the healing of the paralysed man at Capernaum. They recorded it to point out that Jesus was seen by the people to be fulfilling Isaiah's prophesy about the promised Messiah healing the sick. The story tells us that Jesus was preaching . . .

And many were gathered together, so that there was no longer any room. And they came bringing a paralytic. And when they could not get near him because of the crowd, they removed the roof above and let down the pallet on which the paralytic lay. And when Jesus saw their faith, he said to the paralytic:

JESUS: *'My son, your sins are forgiven.'*

STORY-TELLER: *Now some of the Scribes were sitting there, questioning in their hearts, 'Why does this man speak thus? It is blasphemy! Who can forgive sins but God alone?' And immediately Jesus perceiving in his spirit that they thus questioned within themselves, said to them:*

JESUS: *'Why do you question thus in your hearts? Which is easier, to say to the paralytic, "Your sins are forgiven you", or "Rise, take up your bed and walk?" But that you may know the Son of man has authority on earth to forgive sins . . . I say rise, take up your bed and go home!'*

STORY-TELLER: *And he rose, and immediately took up his bed and went out before them all.*

INTERPRETER: 'Son of man' is an old biblical phrase meaning simply, 'man'. However, by this time, it had also come to mean the 'Messiah'. Jesus uses it here so that it could mean either, as a deliberate 'double entendre', baiting the Scribes. Obviously, he could not yet claim in public to be the Messiah, for that would mean certain death for blasphemy. What annoyed the Scribes was not only his claim to 'forgive sins', but his implication that the old Judaic ideas that all suffering came as a result of sin were wrong. It was probably touch and go – but the Scribes decided to wait for a better occasion to deal with him.

[1]See Appendix I. 'The dates and authorship of the gospels': synoptic means 'written from the same general point of view' and applies to Matthew, Mark and Luke, who use the same sources for much of their gospels.

Jesus' Sermon on the Mount

NEW TESTAMENT SCENE 7

The Sermon on the Mount

(St Matthew 5–7. See also Luke 6 & 11)

STORY-TELLER: Great crowds followed Jesus from Galilee and *seeing the crowds he went up on the mountain, and when he had sat down, his disciples came to him. And he opened his mouth and taught them.* The words he spoke, summarised by St Matthew, are known as the 'Sermon on the Mount'. We see him here as he sits down, then as he stands and talks and finally as he kneels above Lake Galilee to pray. Sir Winston Churchill once described this sermon as *'the last word in Christian ethics'.*[1]

JESUS: *'Blessed are the poor in spirit, for theirs is the kingdom of heaven. Blessed are they that mourn, for they shall be comforted. Blessed are the meek, for they shall inherit the earth. Blessed are those who hunger and thirst for righteousness, for they shall be satisfied. Blessed are the merciful, for they shall obtain mercy. Blessed are the pure in heart, for they shall see God. Blessed are the peacemakers, for they shall be the sons of God. Blessed are they who are persecuted for righteousness' sake, for theirs is the kingdom of heaven. Blessed are you when men revile you and persecute you on my account. Rejoice and be glad, for your reward is great in heaven.'*

'You are the salt of the earth. You are the light of the world.'

'Think not that I am come to destroy the law, or the prophets: I am not come to destroy, but to fulfil, I say to you, till heaven and earth pass away, not an iota, not a dot, will pass from the law until all is accomplished.'[2]

'But unless your righteousness exceeds that of the Pharisees, you will not enter the kingdom of heaven.'

'If your right hand causes you to sin, cut it off. If any one strikes you on the right cheek, turn to him the other also.[3] *If any one forces you to go one mile, go with him two. Love your enemies and pray for those who persecute you. For if you love (only) those who love you, what reward have you? Be perfect as your Father in heaven is perfect.'*

'When you give alms to charity, give them in secret; and your Father, who sees in secret, will reward you. Do not lay up for yourselves treasures on earth where mot and rust do corrupt, and thieves break in; but lay up for yourselves treasure in heaven. For where your treasure is, there will your heart be also. You cannot serve God and Mammon.'

'Judge not, that you be not judged. Why do you see the speck in your brother's eye, but do not notice the log that is in your own eye? First take the log out of your own eye, and then you will see clearly to take the speck out of your brother's eye.'

'In praying, do not heap empty phrases. Pray like this: "Our Father, who art in heaven, hallowed be thy name, thy kingdom come, thy will be done, on earth as it is in heaven . . ." Ask and it shall be given you; seek and you shall find; knock and it will be opened to you.'

'WHATEVER YOU WISH THAT MEN WOULD DO TO YOU, DO SO TO THEM: FOR THIS IS THE LAW AND THE PROPHETS.'

'Every man who hears these words of mine, and does them will be like a wise man who built his house on the rock, and every one who does not do them, will be like a foolish man who built his house upon the sand.'

[1]Said to Field Marshal Viscount Montgomery and Sir Anthony Eden. Quoted in 'The Fringes of Power: Vol. II. Sir John Colville; his diary for May 18th 1952. Sir W.S.C. may have been quoting his friend Raymond Asquith, killed on the Somme in 1916.
[2]Matt. 5/17. Also see Romans 13/10 *'Love is fulfilling the Law'.*
[3]i.e. with the object of shaming the aggressor.

Jesus Heals the Roman Centurion's Servant and Raises Jairus' Daughter from the Dead

I have not found so great faith, no, not in Israel

She is not dead but sleeping

NEW TESTAMENT SCENE 8

Jesus Heals the Roman Centurion's Servant and Raises Jairus' Daughter from the Dead

(St Matthew 8. Also Luke 7, 8 and Matthew 9)

STORY-TELLER: After giving his Sermon on the Mount, Jesus returned to Capernaum and was met by a Roman Centurion who said to him:

CENTURION: *'Lord, my servant is lying paralysed at home, in terrible distress.'*

JESUS: *'I will come and heal him.'*

CENTURION: *'Lord, I am not worthy to have you come under my roof, but say the word, and my servant will be healed.'*[1]

JESUS: *'Truly, I say to you, not even in Israel have I found such faith. Go; be it done for you as you have believed.'*

STORY-TELLER: *And the servant was healed from that very moment.*

The second picture illustrates one of two other miracles in which Jesus healed a woman and then raised a dead girl to life. (Luke 8/40 on):

There came a man named Jairus, a ruler in the synagogue; and falling at Jesus' feet he begged him to come to his house, for he had an only daughter, about twelve years of age, and she was dying.

Jesus said nothing, but walked on through the crowd that surrounded him. Then a woman, who had had a flow of blood for twelve years and who could not be healed, came up behind him and touched the hem of his garment. Her flow of blood ceased. Jesus said to Peter, who was with him:

JESUS: *'Who was it that touched me?'*

PETER: *'Master, the multitudes surround you and press upon you.'*

JESUS: *'Someone touched me, for I perceive that power has gone from me.'*

STORY-TELLER: The woman who came trembling, and falling down before him declared in front of everyone why she had touched him, and that she had been healed immediately.

JESUS: *'Daughter, your faith has made you well, go in peace.'*

STORY-TELLER: While he was speaking a man from Jairus' house came and said:

MESSENGER: *'Your daughter is dead. Do not trouble the Teacher any more.'*

JESUS: *'Do not fear, only believe, and she shall be well.'*

STORY-TELLER: Jesus went to Jairus' house and entered the dead girl's room, saying:

JESUS: *'Do not weep, for she is not dead but sleeping.'*

STORY-TELLER: Taking her by the hand he called:

JESUS: *'Child, arise.'*

STORY-TELLER: And her spirit returned, and she got up at once.

[1] This phrase is used in the Communion prayer, as the Priest kneels down at the Lord's Table:
'We are not worthy . . . but thou are the same Lord, whose property is always to have mercy.'

NEW TESTAMENT SCENE 9 *Jesus Calms the Wind and the Waves*

(St Mark 4. Also see St Matthew 8 & St Luke 8)

STORY-TELLER: Once again, all three synoptic gospels tell this story, though they put it in different parts of their record. In this scene, we use the words of St Mark describing Jesus and the disciples as they sail across Lake Galilee:

A great storm arose, and the waves beat into the boat, so that the boat was already filling. But Jesus was in the stern, asleep on a cushion; and they woke him and said to him:

DISCIPLES: *'Teacher, do you not care if we perish?'*

STORY-TELLER: *He awoke and rebuked the wind, and said to the waves,*

JESUS: *'PEACE! BE STILL!'*

STORY-TELLER: *And the wind ceased, and there was a great calm. He said to them:*

JESUS: *'Why are you afraid? Have you no faith?'*

STORY-TELLER: *And they were filled with awe, and said to one another,*

DISCIPLES: *'Who then is this, that even wind and sea obey him?'*

INTERPRETER: It can be seen, from the way that the disciples addressed Jesus and from what they said about him, that they still did not realise who he was. Both St Mark and St Matthew make a point of emphasising in their gospels that Jesus' 'Messiahship' was secret, until much later, when he knew the time had come to reveal himself to them. Secrecy was essential if Jesus was to avoid being killed for blasphemy.

The evangelists probably recorded this and the two previous stories of miracles to show that Jesus was Lord over the gentiles, the dead and the elements as well as being Lord of the chosen people, the Jews.

Jesus and His 12 Disciples – The Sower – The Feeding of the 5,000

NEW TESTAMENT SCENE 10 *Jesus Chooses 12 Apostles: The Parable of the Sower: The Feeding of the 5,000*

(*'The Twelve'*: Matthew 10, 11; Mark 6; Luke 9. *'Sower'*: Matthew 13; Mark 4; Luke 8. *'5,000'*: Matthew 14; Mark 6; Luke 9; John 6)

INTERPRETER: These three scenes show the choosing of the twelve apostles, the parable of the sower and the miracle of the feeding of the '5,000'. An 'apostle' is one who is 'commissioned by the king to fulfil a mission'. Later, the definition 'apostle' comes to mean 'witness'.

STORY-TELLER: *The names of the twelve apostles are these: First, Simon, who is called Peter, and Andrew his brother; James the son of Zebedee and John his brother; Philip and Bartholomew; Thomas and Matthew the tax collector; James the son of Alphaeus, and Thaddaeus, Simon the Canaanite, and Judas Iscariot, who betrayed him. These twelve Jesus sent out, charging them:*

JESUS: *'Preaching as you go, saying the "kingdom of heaven is at hand". Heal the sick, raise the dead. Behold, I send you out as a sheep among wolves; be wise as serpents and innocent as doves. Beware of men; for they will deliver you up to councils, and flog you in the synagogues, and you will be dragged before the governors and kings for my sake. When they deliver you up, be not anxious how you are to speak; for what you say will be given you in that hour; for it is not you who speak, but the Spirit of the Father speaking through you. You will not have gone through all the towns of Israel before the Son of Man comes.'*[1]

STORY-TELLER: While the apostles were away on their mission, Jesus received messengers from John the Baptist, whom Herod[2] had imprisoned and was about to execute. John asked Jesus if he was *'he who is to come, or look we for another?'* Jesus acknowledged indirectly who he was – then he gave a strong hint of his Messiahship – he said that John was 'Elijah', who had come back for them, for Elijah was to reappear before the Messiah came. To emphasise his meaning, he said: *'He who has ears let him hear.'* Jesus also told the people: *'Come unto me, all you who labour and are heavy laden, and I will give you rest. Take my yoke upon you, and learn from me; for I am gentle and lowly of heart, and I will find rest for your souls.'*[3]

While the apostles were still away preaching on their mission, Jesus told the crowds a parable about a sower sowing seed. Some seed fell on good ground, some on rough ground, some among thorns. Only the seed that fell on good ground flourished. Jesus then explained the meaning of his story:

JESUS: *'The seed is the word of God.'* (Not everyone listens – some hear and weaken – others hear and keep faith.)

STORY-TELLER: When the apostles returned, and after Jesus had been teaching to a large crowd until late in the day, he told the apostles to feed the crowd. Their number was about 5,000. They replied: *'We have no more than five loaves and two fishes.'* Jesus took this food, broke and blessed it. The apostles then gave it to the people who ate and were satisfied. Jesus later explained the significance of this, saying: *'I am the bread of life; he who comes to me shall not hunger; and he who believes in me shall not thirst.'*[4]

Jesus also said: *'No one can come to me unless the Father who sent me draws him; and I will raise him up at the last day.'*[5]

Later Jesus repeated his miracle with a crowd of 4,000.

[1] The words *'before the Son of man comes'* raise a mystery. Did Jesus mean the kingdom would have come? – hardly – for that event did not occur. Some scholars suggest he implied that the kingdom would already have come in the sense that his mission and the Age of Christ had begun – the Age of the Church would then follow. [2] Herod Antipas, son of Herod the Great. [3] Matt 11/28. [4] John 6/35. John sets his scene at the Passover. He implies that this miracle was a case of the people being spiritually filled. His gospel mentions three Passovers – suggesting Jesus' mission lasted three years. The other gospels mention only one Passover – at the end. These gospels therefore imply his ministry lasted only eleven or twelve months. [5] John 6/44.

O man of little faith
why did you doubt?

NEW TESTAMENT SCENE 11 *Jesus Walks on Water and Tests Peter's Faith: The Conditions of Discipleship*

(St Matthew 14 and John 6/19. Also Matthew 10/34 on and Luke 14/27 on)

STORY-TELLER: After feeding the 5,000, Jesus *made the disciples get into a boat and go before him to the other side (of the lake). And after he had dismissed the crowds, he went up on the mountain by himself to pray.*

When evening came, he was there alone, but the boat by this time was many furlongs distant from the land, beaten by the waves; for the wind was against them. And in the fourth watch of the night, he came to them, walking on the sea.

But when the disciples saw him walking on the sea, they were terrified, saying,

DISCIPLES: *'It is a ghost!'*

STORY-TELLER: *But, immediately, he spoke to them saying:*

JESUS: *'Take heart, it is I; have no fear.'*

STORY-TELLER: *And Peter answered him:*

PETER: *'Lord, if it is you, bid me come to you on the water.'*

JESUS: *'Come!'*

STORY-TELLER: *So Peter got out of the boat and walked on the water and came to Jesus; but when he saw the wind, he was afraid, and beginning to sink he cried out:*

PETER: *'Lord, save me!'*

STORY-TELLER: *Jesus immediately reached out his hand and caught him, saying to him:*

JESUS: *'O man of little faith, why did you doubt?'*

STORY-TELLER: *And when they got into the boat the wind ceased. And those in the boat worshipped him, saying:*

PASSENGERS: *'Truly you are the Son of God.'*

STORY-TELLER: Shortly after this episode, Jesus came to a turning point in his ministry and revealed many new things, especially how stark and all embracing were his conditions for true discipleship – those of being 'Born anew', of forsaking anyone and anything that comes between us and him, of taking up his cross and following him. His words on this will help to underline the message of the next two scenes.

JESUS: *'Do not think I have come to bring peace on earth, I have come not to bring peace, but a sword. For I have come to set a man against his father, and a daughter against her mother, and a daughter-in-law against her mother-in-law; and a man's foes will be those in his own household.*

He who loves father or mother more than me is not worthy of me. HE WHO DOES NOT TAKE UP HIS CROSS AND FOLLOW ME IS NOT WORTHY OF ME. He who finds his life shall lose it, and he who loses his life for my sake will find it.'

INTERPRETER: This uncompromising approach is meant to shake our natural complacency. Love of God, the First Commandment, MUST come first. Love is our response to him.

You must be born anew

God is Spirit & those who worship
Him must worship in Spirit & Truth

NEW TESTAMENT SCENE 12 *Nicodemus Visits Jesus at Night: Jesus & the Woman of Samaria at the Well*

(St John 3 and 4)

STORY-TELLER: *There was a man of the Pharisees, named Nicodemus, a ruler of the Jews. This man came to Jesus by night and said to him:*

NICODEMUS: *'Rabbi, we know you are a teacher come from God; for no one can do these signs that you do, unless God is with him.'*

JESUS: *'Truly, truly, I say to you, unless one is born anew,[1] he cannot enter the kingdom of God.'*

NICODEMUS: *'How can a man be born when he is old?'*

JESUS: *'Are you a teacher of Israel, and yet you do not understand this? Truly, truly, we speak of what we know, and bear witness to what we have seen; but you do not receive the testimony. If I have told you earthly things and you do not believe, how can you believe if I tell you heavenly things?'*

INTERPRETER: Nicodemus was a secret disciple of Jesus. He spoke in his defence in the council, when the Pharisees were plotting to kill him. At the end, Nicodemus helped Joseph of Arimathaea to bury him. By 'born anew', Jesus meant 'reborn spiritually'.

STORY-TELLER: Immediately after telling this story of Nicodemus, St John tells the story of how Jesus sat by a well in a town of Samaria and asked a woman there for a drink of water:

WOMAN: *'How is it that you, a Jew, ask a drink of me, a woman of Samaria?'*

JESUS: *'If you knew the gift of God, and who it is that is saying "Give me a drink", you would have asked him, and he would have given you living water.'*

WOMAN: *'Sir, you have nothing to draw with, and the well is deep; where do you get that living water?'*

JESUS: *'God is spirit, and those who worship him must worship in spirit and in truth.'*

WOMAN: *'I know the Messiah is coming (he who is called Christ); when he comes, he will show us all things.'*

JESUS: *'I who speak to you am he.'*

[1]See also St Paul and St Peter on this:–
II Cor. 5/17: *'If any one is in Christ, he is a new creation.'*
Romans 6/4: *'We should walk in newness of life.'*
I Peter 1/3: *'By his great mercy we have been born anew to a living hope.'*

You are Peter and upon this rock I will build my Church.

This is my Beloved Son; hear Him.

Go and do likewise

NEW TESTAMENT SCENE 13 *Jesus Says He is Christ & Chooses Peter to Found the Church: The Transfiguration: The Parable of the Good Samaritan*

(Matthew 16 & 17, Mark 8, Luke 10)

INTERPRETER: Jesus has now finished his public teaching to the crowds. He has taken his disciples to the extreme north of Palestine at Caesarea Philippi. He there asks his disciples:–

JESUS: *'Who do men say the "Son of man" is?'*

DISCIPLES: *'Some say John the Baptist, others say Elijah, and others Jeremiah or one of the prophets.'*

JESUS: *'But who do you say I am?'*

PETER: *'You are Christ, the Son of the living God!'*

JESUS: *'Blessed are you Simon Bar-Jona. For flesh and blood has not revealed this to you, but my Father who is in heaven. I tell you you are Peter, and on this rock I will build my church, and the powers of death shall not prevail against it. I will give you the keys of the kingdom of heaven.'*

STORY-TELLER: *Then he strictly charged the disciples to tell no one that he was the Christ. From that time Jesus began to show his disciples that he must go to Jerusalem and suffer many things from the elders and chief priests and scribes, and be killed, and on the third day be raised.*

PETER: *'God forbid, Lord! This shall never happen to you!'*

JESUS: *'Get behind me, Satan! You are a hindrance to me; for you are not on the side of God, but of men!'*

STORY-TELLER: *After six days Jesus took with him Peter and James and John his brother, and led them up a high[1] mountain apart. And he was transfigured before them, and his face shone like the sun, and his garments became white as light. And behold, there appeared to them Moses and Elijah talking with him. (Then) a bright cloud overshadowed them, and a voice from the cloud said:*

VOICE: *'This is my beloved Son, with whom I am well pleased, listen to him.'*

STORY-TELLER: *As they were coming down the mountain, Jesus commanded them:*

JESUS: *'Tell no one of the vision, until the Son of man is raised from the dead.'*

STORY-TELLER: After that, Jesus and his disciples set off in the direction of Jerusalem, many days journey to the south. On the way, a lawyer stood up to put him to the test, saying:

LAWYER: *'Teacher, what shall I do to inherit eternal life?'[2]*

JESUS: *'What is written in the Law?'*

LAWYER: *'You shall love the Lord your God and your neighbour as yourself; but who is my neighbour?'[3]*

STORY-TELLER: Jesus told him of a man who was robbed and left to die by the roadside. A Levite and also a priest saw him, but passed on the other side. Then a Samaritan came, bound up his wounds, took him to an inn and cared for him. Jesus then asked

JESUS: *'Which of these three, do you think, proved neighbour to the man who fell among thieves?'*

LAWYER: *'The one who showed mercy on him.'*

JESUS: *'Go and do likewise.'*

[1]Probably the 9,000 foot high Mount Hermon.
[2]From Luke 10/25 on.
[3]Refer also to Matt 22/36–40 for the two greatest commandments.

70

NEW TESTAMENT SCENE 14

Jesus Encourages Children: He Raises Lazarus: Parable of the Prodigal Son

(From Mark 10, Matthew 19, John 11 & Luke 15)

INTERPRETER: On his way south, Jesus never missed an opportunity to show who was worthy of the 'kingdom'. Once, the crowds pushed their children forward to touch him but the disciples shooed them away. Jesus said:–

JESUS: *'Let the children come to me, do not hinder them; for to such belongs the kingdom of God. Truly, I say to you, whoever does not receive the kingdom of God as a child shall not enter it.'*

STORY-TELLER: Later on, Jesus learned that Lazarus, brother of his friends Martha and Mary, was dying in Bethany. When he reached the place four days later, Lazarus was dead and buried. According to St John, who alone of the evangelists tells the story, Jesus said to Lazarus's sister, Martha:

JESUS: *'Your brother will rise again.'*

MARTHA: *'I know we will rise again in the resurrection at the last day.'*

JESUS: *'I am the Resurrection and the Life; he who believes in me, though he die, yet shall he live, and whoever lives and believes in me shall never die. Do you believe this?'* (John 11/25)

MARTHA: *'Yes, Lord; I believe you are the Christ, the Son of God, he who is coming into the world.'*

STORY-TELLER: Then Jesus went to the tomb and prayed. Then he cried out:

JESUS: *'LAZARUS . . . COME OUT!'*

STORY-TELLER: The dead man came out, his hands and feet bound with bandages and his face wrapped in a cloth. Jesus said to them:

JESUS: *'Unbind him and let him go!'*

STORY-TELLER: Later on, Jesus, according to St Luke, told a parable about a Prodigal Son. Jesus told how a rich man's son was given his inheritance by his father and then left home and squandered it all. He was then so poor that he had to become a swineherd to get anything to live on. Eventually, the son returned home intending to ask his father to treat him as a hired servant. When he was within sight of his home, his father saw him and ran to embrace him and, as he did so, the son said:

PRODIGAL SON: *'Father I have sinned against heaven and before you; I am no more worthy to be called your son.'*

STORY-TELLER: His father was so glad to see him again that he told his servants to prepare a feast of welcome – *'bring the fatted calf and kill it'*. The older son who had worked for his father for many years and had not been given even a small party as a reward was angry and jealous. The father then said to him:

FATHER: *'All that is mine is yours. It was fitting to make merry and be glad, for this your brother was dead, and is alive; he was lost, and is found.'*

INTERPRETER: The real point of the story comes at the end, for it shows how good the father was in dealing with both his sons – it is the story of the 'Good Father' rather than the 'Prodigal Son'.

It is easier for a camel ....than for a rich man to enter the Kingdom

Zachaeus sought to see who Jesus was

NEW TESTAMENT SCENE 15 *The Rich Young Man and the Difficulty*
of Entering the Kingdom:
Jesus Meets Zachaeus

(Mark 10, Luke 19)

STORY-TELLER: A rich young man came to Jesus and asked what he must do to inherit eternal life, as he had obeyed all the commandments of the law. Jesus told him:

JESUS: *'You lack one thing, go and sell all that you have and give to the poor, and you will have treasure in heaven; and come, follow me.'*

STORY-TELLER: *At this his countenance fell, and he went away sorrowful; for he had many possessions. And Jesus looked around and said to his disciples:*

JESUS: *'How hard it will be for those who have riches to enter the kingdom of God! It is easier for a camel to go through the eye of a needle than for a rich man to enter the kingdom of God.'*

INTERPRETER: This does not mean that Jesus disapproved of 'wealth' or 'wealth creation'. He wanted to warn of 'the spiritual dangers' of becoming fanatically attached to money-making, as he realised was the case with this young man. It is only in such an extreme case that Jesus' command 'to sell all' applies – as the following story shows.

STORY-TELLER: There is another aspect of Jesus' teaching on this in a description of his meeting with the rich tax-collector, Zachaeus, as he entered Jerusalem for the last time (Luke 19):–

Zachaeus sought to see who Jesus was but could not, on account of the crowd, because he was small of stature. So he ran ahead and climbed up into a sycamore tree to see him. And when Jesus came to the place, he looked up and said to him:

JESUS: *Zachaeus, make haste and come down; for I must stay at your house today.'*

STORY-TELLER: *And when they saw it they murmured: 'He has gone in to be the guest of a sinner.' And Zachaeus stood and said to the Lord:*

ZACHAEUS: *'Behold, Lord, the half of my goods I will give to the poor; and if I have defrauded any one of anything, I restore it fourfold.'*

INTERPRETER: Jesus saw that wealth was not over-important to Zachaeus, and said to him:–

JESUS: *'Today salvation has come to this house, since he also is a son of Abraham. For the Son of man came to seek and to save the lost.'*

NEW TESTAMENT SCENE 16   *Jesus as the Light of the World*

(John 8)

INTERPRETER: Jesus made several important references to himself and his relationship with God the Father. He twice referred to himself in the words of Isaiah's prophecy as the 'Light of the World'. The first time he did this was shortly after feeding the 5,000, according to St John, who records that he then said:

JESUS: *'I am the Light of the World; he who follows me will not walk in darkness, but will have the light of life.'*

STORY-TELLER: At that time, he answered a Pharisee's question: *'Where is your father'*, by saying:

JESUS: *'You know neither me nor my Father, if you knew me you would know the Father also. If you continue in my word, you are truly my disciples, and you will know the truth, and the truth will make you free. I do nothing on my own authority but speak thus as the Father taught me. Before Abraham was I AM.'* (John 8/12–58)

INTERPRETER: By 'free', Jesus means 'free from the bondage of sin and free from being too worldly'.

By his reference to 'Before Abraham, I AM', Jesus means something far more profound. He meant that, because he was one with the Father, he was 'I AM', that is 'YAHWEH', as we saw with the scene of Moses before the burning bush. In other words, Jesus is saying that in a special way he has existed since before the Creation: 'I AM existence itself!'[1]

STORY-TELLER: Immediately after he said this, the Pharisees realised he was claiming to be God, and so took up stones to kill him: *'but Jesus hid himself, and went out of the temple'*.

INTERPRETER: In saying these things, Jesus was reminding his listeners of the Lord's final promise to Moses, given in the Book of Deuteronomy:

'I will raise up a prophet like you among your brethren; AND I WILL PUT MY WORDS IN HIS MOUTH AND HE WILL SPEAK ALL THAT I COMMAND HIM.'[2]

In the next scene, we shall see that Jesus also made even more pointed remarks concerning his precise relationship with the Father.

[1]St Paul in Colossians 1/15–20 (*c.*60 AD) also wrote on this and amplified the concept of Jesus having existed since before the Creation – also described in St John's gospel 1/2–4. Here St Paul calls Jesus *'The image of the invisible God, the first-born of all creation; for in him all things were created, in heaven and earth, visible and invisible . . . all things were created through him and for him . . . in him all the fullness of God was pleased to dwell.'* Once again, as in St John, Jesus is described as the agent of creation.

[2]Deut. 18/18. Also see page 19 above and John 5/46:– *'If you believed in Moses, you would believe me, for he wrote of me.'*

NEW TESTAMENT SCENE 17

Jesus – The Good Shepherd

(John 10)

STORY-TELLER: St John also tells us how Jesus described himself as the 'Good Shepherd', the traditional image that the Jews used to describe the way God looked after them as his special flock. Jesus now enlightens them on the meaning of this:–

JESUS: *'Truly, truly, I say to you, I am the door of the sheep. If any one enters by me, he will be saved, and I will go in and out and find pasture. I came that they may have life and have it abundantly, I am the GOOD SHEPHERD.'*

'He who is a hireling and not a shepherd, whose own the sheep are not, sees the wolf coming and leaves the sheep and flees; and the wolf snatches them and scatters them. He flees because he is a hireling and cares nothing for the sheep.'

'I am the good shepherd; I know my own and my own know me, as the Father knows me and I know the Father; and I lay my life down for the sheep.'

'And I have other sheep, that are not of this flock; I must bring them also, and they will heed my voice. So THERE WILL BE ONE FLOCK, ONE SHEPHERD.'[1]

INTERPRETER: In this same chapter, St John tells how Jesus explained himself and his relationship with God as being even closer than that of Son. This happened when the Jews asked him:

JEWS: *'How long will you keep us in suspense? If you are the Christ, tell us plainly.'*

STORY-TELLER: Jesus then answered them:

JESUS: *'I told you, and you do not believe. The works that I do in my Father's name, they bear witness to me; but you do not believe, because you do not belong to my sheep. My sheep hear my voice, and I know them, and they follow me; and I give them eternal life, and they shall never perish, and no one shall snatch them from my hand. My Father who has given them to me, is greater than all, and no one is able to snatch them out of the Father's hand. I AND THE FATHER ARE ONE.'*

STORY-TELLER: *The Jews took up stones again to stone him. Jesus answered them:*

JESUS: *'I have shown you many good works from the Father; for which of these do you stone me?'*

JEWS: *'It is not for a good work that we stone you but for blasphemy; because you, being a man, make yourself God.'*

JESUS: *'Do you say of him whom the Father consecrated and sent into the world, "You are blaspheming", because I said, "I am the Son of God"?'*

'If I am not doing the works of my Father then do not believe me; but if I do them, even though you do not believe me, believe the works, that you may understand that the Father is in me and I am in the Father.'

STORY-TELLER: *Again they tried to arrest him, but he escaped from their hands.*

[1]John 10/16.

Jesus Enters Jerusalem for the Last Time

Hosanna to the Son of David!

My House shall be called a House of Prayer!

Woe unto you, you blind guides!

NEW TESTAMENT SCENE 18   *Jesus Enters Jerusalem in Triumph*

(Matthew 21–23, Mark 11, Luke 19 & John 12)

INTERPRETER: At last Jesus and his disciples reached the outskirts of Jerusalem about a week before the Passover. Jesus was then thirty-one years old. St Matthew tells us how Jesus said to his disciples:

JESUS: *'Go into the village opposite you, and immediately you will find an ass tied, and a colt with her; untie them and bring them to me. If anyone says anything to you, you shall say, "The Lord has need of them", and he will send immediately.'*

STORY-TELLER: *This took place to fulfil what was spoken by the prophet (Zecharaiah), saying:–*

'Tell the daughter of Zion, Behold, your king is coming to you, humble, and mounted on an ass.'

The disciples went and did as Jesus directed them; they brought the ass and the colt, and put their garments on them, and he sat thereon. Most of the crowd spread their garments on the road, and others cut branches from the trees and spread them on the road. And the crowds that went before him and that followed shouted: 'Hosanna to the Son of David! Blessed is he who comes in the name of the Lord! Hosanna in the highest!'

And when he entered Jerusalem, all the city was stirred, saying, 'Who is this?' And the crowds said 'This is the prophet Jesus from Nazareth in Galilee.'[1]

And Jesus entered the temple of God and drove out all who sold and bought in the temple, and he overturned the tables of the moneychangers and the seats of those who sold pigeons. He said to them:

JESUS: *'It is written, "My house shall be called a house of prayer"; but you make it a den of robbers.'*

STORY-TELLER: Jesus then went and taught in the temple and the Pharisees took counsel how to entangle him. They went and asked him:

PHARISEES: *'Is it lawful to pay taxes to Caesar or not?'*

JESUS: *'Why put me to the test, you hypocrites? Render under Caesar the things that are Caesar's and unto God the things that are God's.'*

STORY-TELLER: Then he addressed the Sadducees, who asked which was the greatest commandment of the law:

JESUS: *'You shall love the Lord your God and you shall love your neighbour as yourself. On these two commandments hang all the laws and the prophets.'*

STORY-TELLER: Then Jesus attacked the Scribes and Pharisees, saying:

JESUS: *'Woe to you, hypocrites! Woe to you blind guides! You tithe mint and dill and cummin, and have neglected the weightier matters of the law, justice, mercy and faith; these you ought to have done, without neglecting the others. Blind guides, straining at a gnat, and swallowing a camel!'*

[1]Matthew emphasises that, though Jesus and the disciples knew he was the Messiah, the crowd thought him a prophet. Their liturgical chants from the psalms were thus just a matter of form, in honour of the approach of the Passover, typical of the enthusiasm of any patriotic crowd, then or later. The words 'Hosanna to the Son of David . . .' came from Psalm 118/26.

NEW TESTAMENT SCENE 19   *Jesus Explains the Power of Prayer*

(Matthew 21)

STORY-TELLER: A few days after his entry into Jerusalem, Jesus saw a figtree by the wayside and, feeling hungry, he went to it but found it was barren, nothing on it but leaves. Jesus said to the tree:

JESUS: *'May you never fruit again!'*

STORY-TELLER: *And the figtree withered at once. When the disciples saw it they marvelled, saying: 'How did the figtree wither at once?'*

JESUS: *'Truly I say to you, if you have faith and never doubt, you will not only do what has been done to this figtree, but even if you say to this mountain, "Be taken up and cast into the sea", it will be done. And whatsoever you ask in prayer, you will receive, if you have faith.'*[1]

INTERPRETER: This story from St Matthew on prayer is backed up by another of his accounts:

JESUS: *'If two of you agree on earth about anything that they ask, it will be done for them in heaven. For when two or three are gathered together in my name, I am in the midst of them.'*

INTERPRETER: St John is even more explicit on this subject of prayer and, in his First Letter, he adds an important proviso:

'This is the confidence that we have in Him, that if we ask anything according to his will, he hears us.'

[1]Matthew 21/18 & 18/19; I Jn 5/14.

Watch therefore you know not what hour the Lord comes

Well done, good and faithful servant

Insomuch as you have done it to the least of these you have done it to me

NEW TESTAMENT SCENE 20 *Jesus' Last Teaching on the 'Kingdom of Heaven':– The Parables of the Ten Virgins, the 'Talents' & of the Righteous*

(Matthew 25)

INTERPRETER: In order to include these three scenes in one picture, Jesus is shown standing on a balcony in Jerusalem with two disciples, looking out on the everyday events in the city. Each of the three stories concerns the 'kingdom' and Jesus related them shortly after he had told his disciples that one day he would come again into the world, and quoted the Book of Daniel to them:

JESUS: *'There will be great tribulation, such as has not been since the beginning of the world until now, no and never will be. Immediately after the tribulation of those days then will appear the sign of the Son of Man in heaven, and they will see the Son of man coming on the clouds of heaven with power and great glory.'*

STORY-TELLER: Jesus then compared the kingdom of heaven to ten maidens who took their lamps to wait for a bridegroom. He was long in coming. Five wise maidens then took their lamps, trimmed them and filled them with oil. The five foolish maidens, who had no oil, were unable to attend the bridegroom when he finally came, as they were locked outside. Jesus gave the moral of the story:–

JESUS: *'Watch therefore, for you do not know the day or the hour.'*

STORY-TELLER: Jesus then told a parable likening the Kingdom of Heaven to a situation in which a man had entrusted his servants with his goods while he was away. On his return, he learned that one servant, to whom he had given five talents, had turned them into ten talents. Another, to whom he had given two talents, had turned them into four talents – while a third servant, to whom he had entrusted one talent, had taken it and buried it in the ground. To the first two, he said:

MASTER: *'Well done, good and faithful servant; you have been faithful over a little, I will set you over much; enter into the joy of your master.'*

STORY-TELLER: Then to the third servant he said:

MASTER: *'You wicked and slothful servant! You should at least have invested my money with the bankers. Take the talent from him, and give it to him who has ten talents. For to everyone who has will be given, and he will have abundance; but from him who has not, will be taken away. Cast the worthless servant into outer darkness; there men will weep and gnash their teeth.'*

STORY-TELLER: Jesus may then have used an ordinary street scene to make his third point about the Day of Judgement. He shows how those who feed the hungry, give drink to the thirsty, welcome the stranger, clothe the naked, visit the sick and the imprisoned, will be told:

JESUS: *'Come, O blessed of my Father, inherit the kingdom prepared for you from the foundation of the earth. Then the righteous will say: "Lord, when did we do these things?" And the King will answer them: "Truly, I say to you, as you did it to the least of my brethren, you did it to me."'*

STORY-TELLER: Finally, according to St Luke, Jesus told the Pharisees, who had asked him when the kingdom would come, he said – probably referring to himself and his mission, though possibly to the mission of the church:–

JESUS: *'The kingdom of God is in the midst of you.'* (Luke 17/21)[1]

[1]See also last paragraph of the Epilogue, p. 132.

The Last Supper

84

NEW TESTAMENT SCENE 21

The Last Supper

(St Matthew 26 & John 14 & 15. See also Mark 14, Luke 22)

STORY-TELLER: When Jesus had finished these parables and explanations about what kind of people would be welcomed into the kingdom, he said to his disciples:

JESUS: *'You know that after two days the Passover is coming, and the Son of man will be delivered up to be crucified. Go into the city to a certain one, and say to him, "The teacher says, My time is at hand; I will keep the Passover at your house with my disciples."'*

STORY-TELLER: *Then the chief priests and the elders of the people gathered in the palace of the high priest, who was called Caiaphas, and took counsel together in order to arrest Jesus by stealth and kill him. But they said, 'Not during the feast, lest there be a tumult among the people.'*

STORY-TELLER: *Then one of the twelve, who was called Judas Iscariot, went to the chief priests and said.*

JUDAS: *'What will you give me if I deliver him to you?'*

STORY-TELLER: *They paid him thirty pieces of silver. And from that moment he sought an opportunity to betray him.*

Now on the first day of Unleavened Bread (the Thursday), when it was evening, Jesus sat down at table with the twelve disciples; and as they were eating, he said,

'Truly, I say to you, one of you will betray me.'

STORY-TELLER: *They were very sorrowful, and began to say to one another, 'Is it I Lord?' Then, as they were eating, Jesus took the bread, and blessed, and broke it, and gave it to the disciples and said:*

JESUS: *'Take, eat, this is my body. Do this in remembrance of me.'*

STORY-TELLER: *And he took the cup, and when he had given thanks, he gave it to them, saying:*

JESUS: *'Drink of it, all of you, for this is my blood of the covenant, which is poured out for you for the forgiveness of sins. I tell you I shall not drink again of this fruit of the vine until that day when I drink it new*

with you in my Father's kingdom.'

INTERPRETER: In the context of the Passover – a sacrificial meal – Jesus identified the bread with his body and wine with his blood and gave them as symbols through which his disciples would remember the sacrifice he made for them.[1]

STORY-TELLER: According to St John, Judas then went out into the night. John also tells us how Peter boasted that he would *never fall away from Jesus. But Jesus told him:*

JESUS: *'Truly, I say to you, this very night, before the cock crows, you will deny me three times.'*

STORY-TELLER: Peter said he would die with Jesus and not deny him. Then the disciples argued together about which one of them would have the highest place in heaven. Jesus told them:

JESUS: *'In my Father's house there are many mansions; if it were not so, would I have told you that I go to prepare a place for you? I am the way, the truth and the life; no one comes to the Father, but by me. If you had known me, you would have known the Father also; henceforth you know him and have seen him.'*

STORY-TELLER: After Judas had gone, Jesus promised that the Holy Spirit would come to the disciples:

JESUS: *'The counsellor, the Holy Spirit, whom the Father will send in my name, he will teach you all things, and bring to your remembrance all that I have said to you.'* (John 14/25 and 15/26)

[1]'Symbols', and the act of remembrance: All churches who re-enact this sacrifice at the Eucharist, Holy Communion, Lord's Supper or the Mass, regard it as an act of remembrance. However, the Roman Catholic Church regards the bread and wine also as becoming actually, and not merely symbolically, the body and blood of Christ. See 'The Eucharist' on page 111 and also the notes on Thomas Cranmer's life and prayers on page 119, Cardinal Newman on page 124 and Pope John-Paul II on page 128.

NEW TESTAMENT SCENE 22

Jesus' Agony in the Garden

(John 15–18, Luke 22 and see Matthew 26 & Mark 14)

STORY-TELLER: As the supper finished, St John describes how Jesus impressed upon the disciples his doctrine of love:

JESUS: *'If you abide in me, and my words abide in you, ask whatever you will, and it shall be done for you. By this my Father is glorified, that you bear much fruit, and so prove to be his disciples. As the Father has loved me, so have I loved you; abide in my love, just as I have kept my Father's commandments and abide in his love. This is my commandment, that you love one another as I have loved you. Greater love has no man than this, that a man lay down his life for his friends. You are my friends if you do what I command you. You did not choose me, but I chose you and appointed you that you should go and bear fruit and that your fruit should abide; so that whatever you ask the Father in my name, he may give it to you. This I command you, to love one another.'*[1]

STORY-TELLER: Jesus and his disciples then left the city, crossed over the Kidron Valley and entered the garden of Gethsemane on the slopes of the Mount of Olives. There, Jesus said to them:

JESUS: *'You will all fall away because of me this night; for it is written, "I will strike the shepherd and the sheep of the flock will be scattered". But after I am raised up, I will go before you into Galilee.'*[2]

STORY-TELLER: St Luke and St John then tell how Jesus left the disciples to go a little way off and pray alone:

JESUS: *'My Father, if thou art willing, remove this cup from me; nevertheless not my will, but thine be done.'*[3]

'Father, the hour has come; glorify the Son that the Son may glorify thee, since thou hast given him power over all flesh, to give eternal life to all whom thou hast given him. And this is eternal life, that they know thee the only true God, and Jesus Christ whom thou hast sent. I glorified thee on earth having accomplished the work which thou gavest me to do; and now Father, glorify thou me in thy own presence with the glory which I had with thee before the world was made.'[4]

STORY-TELLER: Then Jesus returned to the disciples and found them asleep and said to them:

JESUS: *'Pray that you may not enter into temptation.'*

STORY-TELLER: Jesus went back again to pray, so intensely that *'his sweat became like great drops of blood falling down upon the ground'*.[5] Then, suddenly, Jesus cried out:

JESUS: *'BEHOLD! The hour is at hand, and the Son of man is betrayed into the hands of sinners. Rise, let us be going; see my betrayer is at hand!'*

[1] John 15/7–17.
[2] Matthew 26/30. He quotes Zechariah 13/7.
[3] Luke 22/42.
[4] John 17/1–5.
[5] Luke 22/44. This verse omitted from some modern translations.

NEW TESTAMENT SCENE 23

The Betrayal

(Luke 22. See also Matthew 26, Mark 14 & John 18)

STORY-TELLER: *While Jesus was still speaking, there came a crowd, and the man called Judas, one of the twelve, was leading them. He drew near to Jesus to kiss him; but Jesus said to him:*

JESUS: *'Judas, would you betray the Son of man with a kiss?'*

STORY-TELLER: *And when those who were about him saw what would follow, they said:*

DISCIPLES: *'Lord, shall we strike with the sword?'*

STORY-TELLER: *And one of them struck the slave of the high priest and cut off his right ear. But Jesus said:*

JESUS: *'No more of this! (and he touched his ear and healed him). 'All who take the sword will perish by the sword. Do you think that I cannot appeal to my Father, and he will at once send more than twelve legions of angels? But how then would the Scriptures be fulfilled?'*

STORY-TELLER: Jesus then said to the crowd:

JESUS: *'Have you come out as against a robber, with swords and clubs? When I was with you day after day in the temple, you did not lay hands on me.'*

STORY-TELLER: All this has taken place, that the scriptures of the prophets might be fulfilled. *Then all the disciples forsook him and fled.*[1] *Then those who had seized Jesus led him to Caiaphas, the high priest, where the scribes and the elders had gathered.*[2]

[1]From Matthew 26/56.

[2]According to the three Synoptic gospels, it was now about eleven months since Jesus had begun his ministry. St John's gospel, however, describes events at three Passovers, suggesting that his ministry covered nearly three years. Jesus was therefore between 31 and 33 years old and the date was between 25 and 29 AD taking his birth as being between 4 and 6 BC.

Tell us if you are Christ   I am innocent of this man's blood   Hail King of the Jews

NEW TESTAMENT SCENE 24

Jesus is Tried, Condemned and Crowned with Thorns

(Matthew 26 & 27, Luke 22 & 23, John 18.
See also Mark 14 & 15)

STORY-TELLER: Jesus was taken first to Annas, the father-in-law of the high priest, Caiaphas, and then to Caiaphas and the elders. Peter followed behind the crowd and stood in the doorway as the trial began. He was recognised as a follower of Jesus, but three times denied it: then he heard the cock crow, and he remembered Jesus' words at the supper. Peter then *went out and wept bitterly.*

The chief priests and council sought false testimony against Jesus. At last two came and said:

WITNESS: *'This fellow said: "I am able to destroy the temple of God, and rebuild it in three days."'*

STORY-TELLER: *Jesus was silent. Then the High Priest said:*

CAIAPHAS: *'Have you no answer to make?'* . . . *'By the living God, tell us, are you the Christ, the Son of God?'*[1]

JESUS: *'You have said so. But I tell you, hereafter you will see the Son of man at the right hand of Power, coming on the clouds of heaven.'*

STORY-TELLER: *Then the High Priest tore his robes and said:*

CAIAPHAS: *'He has uttered blasphemy. Why do we still need witnesses? What is your judgement?'*

COUNCIL: *'He deserves death!'*

STORY-TELLER: *When the morning came they delivered him to Pilate the governor.* Pilate heard the charges and asked Jesus:

PILATE: *'Are you King of the Jews?'*

JESUS: *'You have said so. I have come into the world to bear witness to the truth.'*

PILATE: *'What is the truth?'* . . . *'I find no crime in this man.'*

ACCUSERS: *'But he stirs up the people!'*

STORY-TELLER: On hearing that Jesus was a Galilean, Pilate sent him to Herod*, *who was hoping to see some sign done by him. He questioned him, but Jesus made no answer and Herod sent him back to Pilate,* who said:

PILATE: *'I did not find this man guilty, nor did Herod, I will therefore chastise him and release him.'*

CROWD: *'If you release this man you are not Caesar's friend!'*

STORY-TELLER: Pilate then gave the Jews the choice of having Jesus or the robber Barabbas released for the festival, but they cried out:

CROWD: *'Crucify him! Crucify him!'*

STORY-TELLER: *Pilate saw that he was gaining nothing, but rather a riot was beginning. He took water and washed his hands before the crowd, saying:*

PILATE: *'I am innocent of this man's blood; see to it yourselves.'*

STORY-TELLER: The soldiers then took Jesus away, scourged him, robed him in scarlet, crowned him with thorns and mocked him, saying:

SOLDIERS: *'Hail! King of the Jews!'*

---

*Herod Antipas, son of Herod the Great.
[1]Dr Albert Schweitzer (1875–1965), the medical missionary, organist and Bach scholar, suggests in his 'The Quest of the Historical Jesus' that Judas' betrayal may have consisted of informing the High Priests of Jesus' secret claim at Caesaraea Philippi to be the Christ. Caiaphas could not have known otherwise that this was the fatal question to put to Jesus. It is this claim, made in private to the disciples, that may have shocked Judas, our Orthodox Jew, into taking the action he did – and betraying the 'Master'.

Jesus is Crucified and Buried

They compelled Simon of Cyrene to carry His cross

Truly this was the Son of God

As the tomb was close they laid Jesus there

NEW TESTAMENT SCENE 25

The Crucifixion

(Matthew 27, see also Mark 15, Luke 23 and John 19)

STORY-TELLER: *When they had mocked him, they led him away to crucify him. As they went out, they came upon a man of Cyrene, Simon by name; this man they compelled to carry his cross. And when they came to a place called Golgotha (which means the place of the skull), they offered him wine to drink, mingled with gall; but when he had tasted it, he would not drink it.*

And when they had crucified him, they divided his garments among them by casting lots. And over his head they put the charge against him, which read 'This is Jesus the King of the Jews'.[1]

From the sixth hour of the day, until the ninth hour, there was darkness over the land. Then Jesus cried out

JESUS: *'My God! My God! Why hast thou forsaken me?' And a little later he said: 'Father, into thy hands I commit my spirit.'*

INTERPRETER: With these words from the Psalms, which Jesus did not have enough breath to finish, he died. If he had been able to say more and finish the psalms, he would have been able to give these last two messages of hope to his disciples:

PSALMIST: *'Men shall tell of the LORD to coming generations and proclaim his deliverance to a people yet unborn'.*

'Be strong, and let your heart take courage, all you who wait for the LORD.'[2]

STORY-TELLER: As Jesus yielded up his spirit, the curtain of the temple was torn in two: *the earth shook, and the rocks were split. When the centurion and those who were keeping watch over Jesus saw the earthquake and what took place, they were filled with awe and said:*

CENTURION: *'Truly this was the Son of God.'*

STORY-TELLER: St John relates how Jesus, just before his last words, entrusted his mother Mary, who was standing near the cross with Mary Magdalene and[3] Mary the wife of Cleopas, *'to the disciple who he loved'.*[4]

Later, *when it was evening,* a rich man, Joseph of Arimathea, got Pilate's permission to take Jesus' body for burial. *Nicodemus also came, bringing a mixture of myrrh and aloes. They took the body of Jesus, and bound it in linen cloths with spices, and laid it in a new tomb, hewn in the rock, and rolled a great stone to the door of the tomb and departed.'*

[1] In Latin the words were 'IESU NAZARENI REX IUDORUM' ('INRI').

[2] See Psalms 22 & 31 and page 39 above. Quotes Matt 27/46, Lk 23/46.

[3] Or, according to Matthew, 'Mary' (or 'Salome') wife of Zebedee, mother of John and James, perhaps sister to Virgin Mary.

[4] Jesus' last act of entrusting his mother whom he loved to John, his beloved disciple, has an important symbolic meaning for many Christians: Mary, who always believed in her Son (see 'Cana') represents the believing community of the Church. He therefore entrusts her to his 'beloved disciple', John. Though the founder of the Church itself is to be Peter, Mary is to be of special importance to believers. Her eventual title in the early church of *'Theotokos, Mother of God'*, followed naturally from the 4th century dogma of the full deity of Christ. This is also the background for the Catholic communion regarding the Blessed Virgin Mary as mediator between Christ and mankind.

He will be raised on the third day

NEW TESTAMENT SCENE 26

The Risen Christ

(Matthew 27 & 28, John 20. See also Mark 16,
Luke 24 and I Corinthians 15)

INTERPRETER: There were no witnesses inside the tomb where Jesus was buried to record what took place at the moment of his Resurrection. Nor do we know much about the interval between Jesus' burial and the discovery of the empty tomb, with the stone rolled away from the entrance, and Jesus appearing to Mary Magdalene and the disciples, on the Sunday morning, the third day after his death.

During that interval, according to St Matthew, on the Saturday morning, the *chief priests and the Pharisees gathered before Pilate and said:*

JEWS: *'Sir we remember how that impostor said, while he was still alive, "After three days I will rise again." Therefore order the sepulchre to be made secure until the third day, lest his disciples go and steal him away, and tell the people, "He has risen from the dead."'*

PILATE: *'You have a guard of soldiers; go, make it as secure as you can.' So they went and made the sepulchre secure by sealing the stone and setting a guard.*

STORY-TELLER: We hear little more of the guard who seem to have fled from their posts after an earthquake. All we know is that towards dawn on the Sunday, Mary Magdalene went to the sepulchre and *saw that the stone had been taken from the tomb. So she ran and went to Simon Peter and the other disciple, whom Jesus loved, and said:*

MARY MAGDALENE: *'They have taken the Lord out of the tomb, and we do not know where they have laid him.'*

STORY-TELLER: According to St Matthew, Mary Magdalene also saw there had been an earthquake and that an angel had rolled back the stone, who had said:

ANGEL: *'He has risen, as he said. Tell the disciples he has risen from the dead. He is going before you into Galilee.'*

STORY-TELLER: Mark and Luke also describe angels being there. John goes into even greater detail, reporting that the burial cloths had been folded neatly. He also says that, while Peter and the 'other disciple' were examining the tomb, Mary Magdalene stood weeping outside the tomb.

INTERPRETER: None of the disciples had as yet seen Jesus but, within minutes of their arrival at the tomb, Jesus appeared, as we shall see in the next scene, to Mary Magdalene. He must have been changed by his astounding experiences, and he wore different clothes, the burial ones having been left behind.

As St Paul was to write in his First Letter to the Corinthians in about 56 AD, some years before the gospels were written, Jesus was seen on about twelve occasions in different places after his resurrection over a period of forty days. On one such occasion, Paul says that *'he appeared to about five hundred of the brethren at one time, MOST OF WHOM ARE STILL LIVING'.*[1]

STORY-TELLER: The evidence for the Resurrection is, first, the empty tomb; second, the sightings on various occasions; third, experience – it is in tune with nature, for suffering leads to glory. St Paul explains this in I Corinthians 15, which needs to be read in full. The truth of the whole Christian faith turns on the truth of the Resurrection. Easter is its great festival and Sunday is its day of remembrance.

[1]Those who doubt this detailed evidence and whether the tomb was or was not empty must explain how half the Apostles could go to their deaths as martyrs knowing that they had been broadcasting a set of lies. The facts, as presented in the gospels of St Luke and St John, stress the bodily nature of the Risen Christ but, equally, they emphasise the mysterious nature of his actual presence. For example, they tell how he arrives within closed doors and then vanishes at will. Thus, the message about the Risen Christ depicts a physical and spiritual unity rather than a ghostly or visionary one, yet the physical nature of the body is of a most unusual kind.

Woman, why are you weeping?

They had seen a vision of Angels who said he was alive

See, my hands and my feet!

NEW TESTAMENT SCENE 27

Jesus' Appearances After His Resurrection

(Matthew 28, John 20, Luke 24. See also Mark 16)

STORY-TELLER: The news soon spread. According to St Matthew, *some of the guard went to the city and told the chief priests all that had taken place. They gave a sum of money to the soldiers and said, 'Tell the people, "His disciples came by night and stole Him away while we were asleep."'*

Meanwhile, Mary Magdalene was weeping outside the tomb and *she turned round and saw Jesus standing, but she did not know it was Jesus. Jesus said to her:*

JESUS: *'Woman, why are you weeping? Whom do you seek?'*

STORY-TELLER: *Supposing him to be the gardener, she said to him:*

MARY MAGDALENE: *'Sir, if you have carried him away, tell me where you have laid him.'*

JESUS: *'MARY!'*

MARY MAGDALENE: *'RABBONI, TEACHER!'*

JESUS: *'Do not hold me, for I have not yet ascended to my Father!'*

STORY-TELLER: *Mary went and said to the disciples: 'I have seen the Lord!'*

That very day two of them were going to a village named Emmaus, about seven miles from Jerusalem, and talking about these things that had happened. While they were talking Jesus drew near and went with him. But their eyes were kept from recognising him.

He asked what they were talking about. They told him about Jesus of Nazareth, how he was crucified and buried and that women had reported that they had seen a vision and that he was alive. Then Jesus said:

JESUS: *'Was it not necessary that the Christ should suffer these things and enter into his glory?'*

STORY-TELLER: *And beginning with Moses and all the prophets, he interpreted to them in all the scriptures the things concerning himself. So they drew near to the village and they asked him to stay with them. And when he was at table with them, he took the bread and blessed, and broke it and gave it to them. Their eyes were opened and they recognised him; and he vanished.*

They rushed back to Jerusalem and as they were telling the eleven disciples what had happened, Jesus *himself stood with them. They were startled and supposed they had seen a spirit. And Jesus said:*

JESUS: *'Why are you troubled? See my hands and my feet, that it is I myself; handle me, and see; for a spirit has not flesh and bones as you see that I have.'* And he took food and ate before them.

STORY-TELLER: Jesus appeared to the disciples again when, according to St John, Thomas was not present. The disciples told Thomas later that they had seen Jesus but he refused to believe them. Then, when Jesus appeared again and Thomas was present, Thomas actually touched Jesus' wounds and said:

THOMAS: *'My Lord and my God!'*

JESUS: *'Have you believed because you have seen me? Blessed are those who have not seen me and yet believe.'*

NEW TESTAMENT SCENE 28

Jesus' Last Appearances and His Ascension into Heaven

(Matthew 28, Luke 24, John 21, Mark 16 & Acts 1)

STORY-TELLER: The sightings of Jesus were seen for forty days and then his mantle, like that of Elijah, taken by Elisha, had to be taken up by his disciples. He then gave them the power to do this at Pentecost.

In this scene, St Matthew shows us how the disciples went to a mountain in Galilee to which Jesus had directed them. *When they saw him, they worshipped him; but some doubted, and Jesus said to them:*

JESUS: *'All authority in heaven and on earth is given to me. Go therefore and make disciples of all nations, baptizing them in the NAME OF THE FATHER AND OF THE SON AND OF THE HOLY SPIRIT,*[1] *teaching them to observe all that I have commanded; and lo, I AM WITH YOU ALWAYS, TO THE CLOSE OF THE AGE.'*

STORY-TELLER: St Luke describes how, after the encounter on the road to Emmaus and on other occasions, Jesus reminded the disciples that the prophet Hosea had also foretold of his death and of his Resurrection three days later.[2] He also reminded them of his promise to send the 'Comforter' to them when he had gone from them:

JESUS: *'Stay in the city until you are clothed with power from on high.'*

STORY-TELLER: Luke then tells us that Jesus took the disciples as far as Bethany, near Jerusalem, and how he lifted up his hand and blessed. *While he blessed them, he parted from them and was carried up into heaven.*

Mark gives a similar description of Jesus' ascension into heaven and, though John's gospel does not mention it, we read in Acts that *'before many days you shall be baptized with the Holy Spirit . . . and you shall be my witnesses in Jerusalem and in all Judaea and in Samaria and to the end of the earth'. And when he had said this, as they were looking on, he was lifted up, and a cloud took him out of their sight.*

And while they were gazing into heaven as he went, behold two men stood by them in robes of white and said:

ANGELS: *'This Jesus, who was taken up from you into heaven, will come in the same way as you saw him go into heaven.'*

STORY-TELLER: Though John does not describe the Ascension, he does give some of Jesus' last words to the disciples at the lake of Galilee:

JESUS: *'Feed my lambs, tend my sheep.'*

[1]See Matt 28/20 and Appendix III on page 137 for the doctrine of the early church (4th century) on the 'Trinity'.
[2]Hosea 6/1 and 2.

(NB: The Koran denies that Jesus died on the cross – thus avoiding the need for Mahomet to explain away Jesus' post-resurrection appearances.)

They were all filled with the Holy Spirit

This Jesus, God raised up and of that we are all witnesses

Silver & Gold I have none but what I have I give you

NEW TESTAMENT SCENE 29

Pentecost: The Coming of the Holy Spirit: Peter's Miracle

(Acts 2 & 3)

STORY-TELLER: The Feast of Pentecost took place fifty days after the Passover. The Apostles, or 'Witnesses', as Acts describe the disciples, gathered with Matthias, their elected replacement for Judas among the 'Twelve'.

Suddenly a sound came from heaven like the rush of a mighty wind, and it filled the house where they were sitting. And there appeared to them tongues as of fire, distributed and resting on each one of them. And they were filled with the Holy Spirit and began to speak in other tongues, as the Spirit gave them utterance.[1]

This was the 'Comforter' Jesus had promised he would send to them when he spoke of the future at the Last Supper. This also was, in Peter's eyes, the fulfilment of the prophesy made by the Prophet Joel. Peter therefore spoke to the people outside who were amazed at the way these men of Galilee could suddenly speak in so many different languages:

PETER: *'Men of Judaea and all who dwell in Jerusalem, give ear to my words. These men are not drunk as you suppose; but this is what was spoken by the prophet Joel:*

"And in the Last Days it shall be, God declares, that I will pour out my Spirit upon all flesh and your sons and daughters shall prophesy, and your young men shall see visions, and your old men shall dream dreams. And I will show wonders in the heaven above and signs on the earth beneath."'

STORY-TELLER: Peter then taught the crowd about Jesus and converted some three thousand souls who came to be baptized. The Apostles then continued to teach daily and spent their time together in fellowship and in *'breaking of bread and prayers'*. They thus began to carry out Our Lord's command at the Last Supper to *'do this in remembrance of me'*, the first celebrations of the 'Eucharist' or the sacrifice of 'Thanksgiving'.

On one of these days, as Peter and John were walking towards the gate of the temple of God called 'Beautiful', they were asked for alms by a crippled beggar. Peter said to him:

PETER: *'Silver and gold have I none; but I give you what I have: In the name of Jesus Christ of Nazareth, WALK!'*

And, immediately, his feet and ankles were made strong and he leapt up, stood and walked, and entered with them into the temple, walking and leaping and praising God. All the people then ran together towards them, greatly wondering. And as the lame man who had been healed clung to Peter and John, Peter addressed the people and again told them about Jesus, who had been raised from the dead. He told them that it was he of whom God spoke to Moses when he told him: 'I will raise a prophet from among your brethren, like unto me.'

[1]This is the climax of the New Testament Story and indeed of the whole Bible, for with the coming of the Holy Spirit, the Trinity of God, the Father, God the Son, (who is the earthly image of God) and of God the Holy Spirit was complete. See notes in Appendix III.

'Lord Jesus, receive my Spirit'

'Saul, Saul, why do you persecute me?'

Faith, Hope, Love abide the greatest of these is Love.

NEW TESTAMENT SCENE 30   *Martyrdom of Stephen: Conversion of St Paul: Paul's 1st Letter to the Corinthians*

(Acts 6–9, 17; I Corinthians 13)

STORY-TELLER: The apostles had elected Stephen as a Deacon to help manage the affairs of the growing church. Stephen was *'full of grace and power and did great wonders and signs among the people'*, but he was arrested on false charges of blasphemy and was dragged out of the city by the Jews and was stoned to death. As he fell dying, he cried out:

STEPHEN: *'Lord do not hold this sin to their charge.'*

STORY-TELLER: A man called Saul, who was an ardent persecutor of the Christians, watched the stoning. Then he was sent with letters to Damascus to persecute the Christians. On the way there, *suddenly a light from heaven flashed about him. And he fell to the ground and heard a voice saying:*

'VOICE': *'Saul, Saul, why do you persecute me?'*

SAUL: *'Who are you Lord?'*

'VOICE': *'I am Jesus, whom you are persecuting; but rise and enter the city and you will be told what to do.'*

STORY-TELLER: Saul, who had been blinded by the light, was led to Damascus, where a Christian, named Ananias, was told by the Lord in a vision to go to Saul in a street called 'Straight'. Ananias did so and first cured Saul's blindness; later, he baptized him as a Christian. Then in the synagogues Saul proclaimed Jesus, saying – *'He is Son of God.'*[1] Some time later, Saul met the apostles in Jerusalem. They accepted him and renamed him 'Paul'.

Paul, accompanied by Barnabas, went to preach the gospel in Antioch, where he met Mark, the future evangelist. He and Barnabas then taught in Cyprus, Macedonia, Athens and Corinth. In Athens, Paul saw an altar dedicated *'To an unknown god.'* Paul then explained to the Athenians:

PAUL: *'What you worship as "unknown", this I proclaim to you. The God who made the world and everything in it, being the Lord of heaven and earth, does not live in shrines built by men. He made men to live on the face of the earth, that they should seek God, in the hope that they might feel after him and find him. Yet he is not far from each one of us for "In him we move and have our being."'*

STORY-TELLER: Paul then told them that God had now fixed a day of Judgement and all men will be raised from the dead. The Athenians were intrigued and said: *'We will hear you again about this.'*[2]

INTERPRETER: Years later, after Paul had established a church in Corinth, he wrote to the congregation there, saying:

PAUL: *'If I speak with the tongues of men and angels, but have not love, I am a noisy gong or a clanging cymbal. If I have prophetic powers, understand all mysteries, and all knowledge, and have all faith, so as to move mountains, but have not love, I am nothing. Love is patient and kind; love is not jealous or boastful; it is not arrogant or rude. Love does not insist on its own way; it is not irritable or resentful; it does not rejoice at wrong, but rejoices at right. Love bears all things, believes all things, hopes all things, endures all things. Love never ends. Faith, hope, Love abide, these three; but the greatest of these is Love.'*[3]

[1] Acts 9/20.

[2] This is described in Acts 17. One other passage in Acts, before this account, is worth recording. This is in chapter 10, which describes St Peter's meeting with the Roman Centurion Cornelius of the Italian Cohort. Verses 34–43 describes St Peter's case for believing in Jesus.

[3] I Cor. 13.

St Paul Commissions St Timothy

Timothy my son, wage the good warfare...as a good soldier of Christ

New Testament Letters
Part One

STORY-TELLER: This picture of St Timothy being sent on his mission to Ephesus by St Paul symbolizes the missionary zeal of all the New Testament letters. Those quoted here are signposts for further reading.

ST PAUL: (I Tim. 1/18 & 6/12, II Tim. 2/3):   *This charge I commit to you, Timothy my son, that you wage the good warfare. Aim at righteousness, godliness, faith, love, steadfastness, gentleness. Fight the good fight of faith; take hold of the eternal life to which you are called. Share in suffering as a good soldier of Christ.*

(Heb. 1/1):   *In many and various ways God spoke of old to our fathers by the prophets; but in these last days he has spoken to us by a Son, whom he appointed heir to all things, through whom he also created the world.*[1]

(Gal. 4/4):   *When the time had come, God sent forth his Son, born of woman under the law, to redeem those under the law, so that they might be adopted as sons.*

(Philippians 2/5–8):   *Christ Jesus who, though he was in the form of God, emptied himself, taking the form of a servant, being born in the likeness of men.* (II Cor. 8/9): *He became poor that by his poverty you might become rich.*

(Rom. 1/16–17):   *The gospel is the power of God for salvation to every one who has faith. For in it the righteousness of God is revealed through faith for faith; as it is written 'He who through faith is righteous shall live.'*[2]

(Rom. 3/23):   *Since all have sinned and fallen short of the glory of God, they are justified*[3] *by grace as a gift, through the redemption which is Christ Jesus, whom God put forward, as an expiation by his blood, to be received by faith.*

(Rom. 5/1):   *Since we are justified by faith, we have peace with God through our Lord Jesus Christ. Through him we have obtained access to this grace in which we stand, and we rejoice in our hope of sharing the glory of God. More than that, we rejoice in our sufferings knowing that suffering produces endurance and endurance produces character, and character produces hope, and hope does not disappoint us, because God's love has been poured into our hearts through the Holy Spirit he has given us.*

(Rom. 8/9–17):   *The Spirit of God dwells in you. The Spirit helps us in our weakness; for we do not know how to pray as we ought, but the Spirit intercedes for us with sighs too deep for words. And he who searches in the hearts of men knows what is in the mind of the Spirit.*

(Rom. 8/18–24):   *The sufferings of the present time are not worth comparing with the glory that is to be revealed to us. For creation waits with eager longing for the revealing of the sons of God; for the creation was subject to futility, not of its own will but by the will of him who subjected it in hope; because creation itself will be set free from the bondage to decay and obtain the glorious liberty of the children of God. We know that the whole creation is groaning in travail together until now; and not only the creation, but we ourselves, who are the first fruits of the Spirit, groan inwardly as we wait for adoption as sons, the redemption of our bodies. For in this hope we are saved.*[4]

INTERPRETER: We should remember that St Paul's letters were written 10 to 15 years before the earliest gospel. They were written to Christian converts and therefore were commentaries on the oral tradition of the Gospel – which was all that was then available. They reveal the depth of the early church's thought well in advance of the most spiritual gospel of all, St John's.

---

[1]'Through whom he created the world' – see Jn 1/3 for reference to this.
[2]From Habakkuk 2/4.
[3]I.e. acquitted of sin.
[4]This suggests Paul believed the redeeming purpose of God includes the whole physical universe, all creatures and, perhaps, even all things, which are not yet perfect. Matthew and Luke imply this also – see Matt. 10/29, Lk. 12/6.

The Ideal Christian Knight

NEW TESTAMENT SCENE 31

New Testament Letters
Part Two

STORY-TELLER: This picture of St George, the ideal Christian knight, symbolises St Paul's advice in his letter to the Ephesians:–

ST PAUL: (Eph. 6/13–17): *Take the whole armour of God, that you may withstand in the evil day, and having done all to stand. Stand therefore having girded your loins with truth, and having put on the breastplate of righteousness, and having shod your feet with the equipment of the gospel of peace; besides all these, taking the shield of faith, with which to quench the flaming darts of the evil one. And take the helmet of salvation and the sword of the Spirit, which is the word of God.*

(Rom. 12/19): *Beloved, never avenge yourselves, but leave it to the wrath of God; for it is written: 'Vengeance is mine, I will repay, says the Lord.'*[1]

(Rom. 14/17): *The kingdom of God is not food and drink, but righteousness and peace and the fellowship of the Holy Spirit.*

(I Cor. 15/3): *Christ died for us according to the scriptures.*[2]

(I Cor. 15/21): *As man came by death,[3] by a man came also the resurrection of the dead. For as in Adam all die, so in Christ shall all be made alive.* (INTERPRETER: Paul sees Christ as a 'Second Adam' – a new creation).

(II Cor. 5/17–21): *If any one is in Christ, he is a new creation;[4] the old has passed away, behold the new has come. For your sake he (God) made him to be sin, so that in him we might become the righteousness of God.*

(Ephes. 4/26 & 5/1): *Be angry but do not sin; do not let the sun go down on your anger, and give no opportunity to the devil. Be imitators of God, as beloved children.* (Rom. 12/1): *Present your bodies as a living sacrifice, wholly acceptable to God.*

(Heb. 11/1–3): *Faith is assurance of things hoped for, for the conviction of things not seen. For by it the men of old received divine approval. By faith we understand that the world was created by the word of God so that what is seen was made out of things which do not appear.* (II Cor. 5/7): *We walk by faith, not by sight.*

(Heb. 13/2): *Let brotherly love continue. Do not neglect to show hospitality to strangers, for thereby some have entertained angels unaware.* (INTERPRETER: Paul here refers to Abraham & Lot, Genesis 18/1–8, 19/1–24).

(Gal. 2/16): *Man is not justified by works of the law, but through faith in Jesus Christ.*

ST JAMES: (2/17): *Faith by itself, if it has no works is dead.* (INTERPRETER: This does not contradict Paul, for we learn from the parable of the 'Talents' (p. 82/83), that we must do what we can – once we have faith).

ST PETER: (I Pet. 1/3 and 1/8): *By his great mercy we have been born anew to a living hope, through the resurrection of Jesus Christ.*[5]

ST JOHN: (I Jn. 2/1 & 4/8): *If anyone does sin, we have an advocate with the Father, Jesus Christ, the Righteous, and he is the expiation of our sins, and not ours only, but the sins of the whole world. He who does not love, does not know God; God is love.* (Also see Rom. 13/10): *Love is the fulfilling of the law.*

ST PAUL: (II Cor. 13/14): *The grace of the Lord Jesus Christ and the love of God and the fellowship of the Holy Spirit be with you all.*

[1]Deuteronomy 32/35.
[2]See Isaiah 53/5–12.
[3]Paul refers to the first murder, by Cain.
[4,5]See also p. 67 reference to 'born anew' in Jesus' talk with Nicodemus.

In the last days the Mountain of the Lord shall be established

Then they shall see the Son of Man coming in the clouds with Great Power and Glory

ARMAGEDDON

And he shall judge the Nations

Behold! I create a New Heaven & a New Earth

Come ye Blessed of my Father inherit the Kingdom

'He Shall Come again with Glory to Judge both the Quick and the Dead'

NEW TESTAMENT SCENE 32

The Last Judgement

STORY-TELLER: We begin this scene – which sums up the main scripture readings on the 'Last Days' at the end of Time – with this quotation from St Paul's First Letter to the Thessalonians:–

ST PAUL: *'We would not have you ignorant brethren concerning those who sleep, that you may not grieve as others do who have no hope. For since we believe that Jesus died and rose again, even so, through Jesus, God will bring with him those who have fallen asleep. For the Lord himself will descend from heaven with a cry of command, with the archangel's call, and with the sound of the trumpet of God. And the dead in Christ will rise first; then we who are alive, who are left, shall be caught up together with them in the clouds to meet the Lord in the air; and so shall we always be with the Lord'* (I Thes. 4/13–18).

INTERPRETER: We illustrate this moment of the general resurrection at the time of Christ's Second Coming. The prophesies of Isaiah and Daniel are given at the top – Mount Zion can be seen beneath them, as the four horses of the apocalypse from the Revelation to John come on stage. On either side, on the horizon, the New Heaven and the New Earth of both Isaiah and Revelation can be seen coming into being. The quotation from Isaiah about this event is in the central panel at the bottom of the picture.

As Christ – Daniel's 'Son of Man' and also as in St Matthew's gospel – comes back to us in glory, there are five scenes beside and beneath him. On the left, as in Isaiah, the nations march to judgement – they pass the flames of Hell and of the battlefield of Armageddon, (from Rev. 16/16). Beneath them, Isaiah's angel *'beats swords into ploughshares and spears into pruning hooks'* (Isaiah 2/4). Beneath the figure of Christ is this scene from Isaiah's prophesy:–

ISAIAH: *'The wolf shall dwell with the lamb, and the leopard shall lie down with the kid, and the calf and the lion and fatling together, and a little child shall lead them. The cow and the bear shall feed, their young shall lie down together, and the lion shall eat straw like the ox. They shall not hurt or destroy in all my holy mountain'* (Isaiah 11/6 & 7).

STORY-TELLER: As these things happen, Christ comes forward and *'every eye shall see him'* (Rev. 1/7) and he will say:–

CHRIST: *'I am Alpha and Omega. Fear not, I am the First and the Last; I have the keys of death and Hades'* (Rev. 1/8).

STORY-TELLER: Meanwhile, St Michael and his angels have destroyed the forces of Antichrist on the field of Armageddon, as in Revelation, from which we get these beautiful words of St John:–

ST JOHN: *'Then I saw a new heaven and a new earth; for the first heaven and the first earth had passed away, and the sea was no more. And I saw the holy city, new Jerusalem, coming out of heaven from God prepared as a bride adorned for her husband; and I heard a loud voice from the throne saying: "Behold, the dwelling of God is with men. He will dwell with them, and they shall be his people, and God himself will be with them; he will wipe away every tear from their eyes, and death shall be no more, neither shall there be mourning nor crying nor pain any more, for the former things have passed away." And he who sat upon the throne said:*

GOD: *'Behold I make all things new. It is done! I am Alpha and Omega, the Beginning and the End. To the thirsty I will give from the fountain of life. He who conquers shall have this heritage and I will be his God and he shall be my son'* (Rev. 21/1–7).

STORY-TELLER: Christ will also summon the 'Righteous' to the seat of Judgement – which is in the heavenly tent, containing both the seat of judgement (see the scales of justice) and also Isaiah's 'Messianic Feast', or the 'Marriage Feast of the Lamb', (from Isaiah 25/6 and Rev. 19/9). Christ will say:–

CHRIST: *'Come ye Blessed of my Father, inherit the Kingdom prepared for you from the foundation of the world'* (Matt. 25/34).

STORY-TELLER: The 'Righteous' can be seen on the right, as groups from all the ages gather and follow martyrs – who are carrying their palms. Beneath them, in the right hand corner, stands the angel blowing the 'last trump', which is described in one of the following readings from St Paul's 1st letter to the Corinthians. All these images in the picture are symbolic, allegorical concepts based on prophetic visions and utterances, for as St Paul wrote:

ST PAUL: *'Now we see in a mirror dimly, but then face to face. Now I see in part, but then I shall understand fully'* (I Cor. 13/12).

'How are the dead raised? With what kind of body do they come? Not all bodies are alike, there are celestial bodies and terrestrial bodies. So it is with the resurrection of the dead. What is sown is perishable; it is sown a physical body, it is raised a spiritual body. Flesh and blood cannot enter the kingdom of heaven' (From I Cor. 15/35–50).

'Lo! I tell you a mystery. We shall not sleep, but shall all be changed in a moment, in a twinkling of an eye, at the last trumpet. For the trumpet shall sound and the dead shall be raised imperishable, and mortals put on immortality. O death where is thy victory? O death where is thy sting?' (From I Cor. 15/51–55).

Note on The Tent: The idea for using a tent to represent the meeting place of the world and heaven came from two sources. First, from Moses' 'Tent of the Meeting' (see page 18) – which is described by St Stephen at his trial as 'The Tent of Witness' (see Acts 7/44). Second, from a 4th century AD fresco in a room beneath the church of SS. Giovanni Paulo on the Caelian hill in Rome. This fresco shows three martyrs, who – after their execution – are seen walking through a tent, the veil between this world and the next, on their way to Paradise. As they move through the tent, their severed heads are restored to their proper place. This concept of a tent also appears in some other early Christian pictures.

NEW TESTAMENT SCENE 33   *The Eucharist – Holy Communion –*
Mass – The Lord's Supper

STORY-TELLER: We end the New Testament by illustrating the Sacraments of the 'Eucharist', or 'Thanksgiving' – the Holy Sacrifice, the Mass or Holy Communion, that re-enact the Last Supper. Below the picture, we have put St Augustine's[1] description – the 'Visible Word' – which St John referred to as the 'Bread of Life'.

The first mention of the Sacrament is in St Paul's 1st Letter to the Corinthians.[2] His words are written round the picture: *'As often as you eat this bread and drink this cup, you proclaim Our Lord's death until he comes.'* These words follow St Paul's reminder to his readers that Jesus had said: *'Do this in remembrance of me'* and *'This cup is the new covenant in my blood.'*

St Paul's letter was written long before the gospels or Acts, but we know from Acts[3] that the members of the early Church regularly met for the *'breaking of bread and prayers'*.

INTERPRETER: This rite of Eucharist or Mass, in remembrance of Jesus, has become the central act of Christian worship – the 'Mystery' at the heart of our religion.

Since the earliest days of the Church, it has been recognised that all who participate in this rite can gain a special sense of spiritual uplift. The attempts to explain this in the middle ages had a divisive influence,[4] although this is less so now than it was. Let us therefore end with the words of an Anglican parish priest,[5] who wrote on this subject:

PRIEST: *Although today Christian churches do think in different ways about this central mystery, we should all, in this act of remembrance, recall that:*

'CHRIST HAS DIED: CHRIST HAS RISEN: CHRIST WILL COME AGAIN.'

In this way, past, present and future are all gathered together in the act of Eucharist. Also, in the consecration of the Sacrament of Bread and

Wine, all the mighty acts of God in Christ are not only remembered, but are brought together:

INCARNATION, LIFE, DEATH, RESURRECTION, ASCENSION, THE GIFT OF THE HOLY SPIRIT, AND HIS COMING AGAIN.

[1]St Augustine (354–430) – see page 114. [2]I Cor. 11/23. [3]Acts 2/42. [4]E.g. The doctrine of Transubstantiation – introduced by the Abbot of Corbie, near Athens, St Paschasius Radbertus (d. 865). He wrote that, at the consecration, the Sacraments of bread and wine really do become the Body and Blood of Christ, and are not just symbolically so. [5]Letter to the author from the Revd Roy Boff MA.

The 'Visible Word' – The Bread & Blood of Life

From St Paul II Corinthians 13, v 14. The last words in his letter.

An Introduction to Prayer with Illustrated Examples from the Earliest Days of the Church until Modern Times

As children, we usually begin our prayers by thanking God for our blessings, then by asking for forgiveness of our sins and forgetfulness. Then we petition God for ourselves and others.

As we get older, we realise that our next great need in prayer is to seek to keep ourselves on the right lines and for strength of moral purpose. St Augustine of Hippo described this kind of prayer as being one *'to elevate us, not to make God change his mind, but to bring us round to what we ought to desire'*.

Prayer is an encounter with God. We need to try to get into tune with him, if we are to receive spiritual guidance. This is not too formidable a task, as we saw with Moses in the Wilderness – he found that the Lord used to speak to him *'face to face, as a man does to his friend'*. Another example of this is how St Teresa of Avila found that prayer was like *'a conversation with Him Who loves us'*. Children seem to understand this easily – as they adopt the conversational approach in prayer quite naturally. They should not be discouraged. The hardest part of prayer is the need for humility and obedience – in saying the Lord's Prayer, we really should mean *'thy will be done'* and so ensure that *'our will is his will'*.[1]

We know from the gospels that our prayers are listened to in heaven. We also know from St John's and St Paul's letters that we have an indwelling spirit which can communicate with God's Holy Spirit. St John wrote that: *'we know he abides in us, by the Spirit which he has given us'*.[2] St Paul wrote – *'The Spirit of God dwells in you'* – *'When we cry Father! It is the Spirit himself bearing witness with our spirit that we are children of God.'*[3]

As we have indicated earlier, the Christian concept of God is a Trinity – Father, Son and Holy Spirit – three persons in One God. This is explained more fully in Appendix III. This doctrine can be found to work quite simply in practice – through its application in the act of prayer. First, it is the Holy Spirit who leads us to pray; second, through our mediator and advocate Jesus Christ, we are brought to the presence of God. Sometimes, even through this approach, we may find ourselves lost for words. Then, if we listen in silence, we may find a dialogue developing to and fro between our spirit and his Spirit.

There is one other great problem in prayer – the unanswered prayer. It seems, too often, that – although our prayers are heard – they are ignored. This happens even when we pray with all humility and devotion for something which seems to be in accordance with God's teaching and will.

We can only offer a partial solution. First, God is normally constrained from intervening miraculously by the nature of his own creation. If he were to intervene – say over disease or natural disasters – he would have to perform yet more miracles subsequently to restore the natural balance. Such a miracle-world would be self-defeating. It could undermine the physical structure on which we rely for our technology. It would also remove the need for us to strive – for research into new medicine – or for any living species to seek survival or perfection through natural selection. Also, in the sense that God has a purpose for us, a miracle-world could make us superfluous. Finally, where evil, tyranny and cruelty are involved – since God has given mankind free-will to do evil as well as good – it is up to us to deal with evil over the long-term ourselves.

The way God does intervene is by giving us strength and hope in answer to our prayers. We need, therefore, to persist in prayer in spite of disappointments. Besides strength and hope, we may also acquire a deeper insight into a purpose that is greater than our own – and a greater sense of selflessness. We may then be able to turn misfortune to good account – as St Paul wrote – *'I can do all things through him who strengthens me.'*[4]

[1] John 7/17.
[2] 1st Letter of John 3/24.
[3] Romans 8/9–16.
[4] Philippians 4/13.

St Augustine of Hippo

Saint Augustine:
'Our hearts are restless till they rest in Thee'.

Almighty God, in whom we live and move and have our being, you who have made us for yourself, so that our hearts are restless till they rest in thee,[1] grant us purity of heart and strength of purpose, so that no selfish passion hinders us from knowing your will, no weakness from doing it; but that in your light we may see clearly, and in your service find perfect freedom; through Jesus Christ our Lord.[2]

Eternal God, who are the light of the minds that know you, the joy of hearts that love you and the strength of the wills that serve you; grant us so to know you, that we may truly love you, and so to love you that we may fully serve you, whom to serve is perfect freedom, in Jesus Christ our Lord.

O God, by your mercy strengthen us, who lie exposed to the rough storms of troubles and temptations. Help us against our own negligence and cowardice, and defend us from the treachery of our unfaithful hearts. Help us we implore you, and bring us to your safe haven of peace and happiness.

*

St Augustine (354–430) was the greatest thinker of the early church. Before his conversion to Christianity, through his mother, St Monica, and St Ambrose, bishop of Milan, he was professor of philosophy at Milan university. His famous Confessions are the public confession of a bishop on his knees. A prolific writer of sermons and prayers, he battled successfully against the prevailing heresies of his day. As he lay dying, the city of Hippo, of which he was both bishop and governor, was besieged by the Vandals, who had taken Rome and swept through Gaul, Spain and North Africa. Hippo was a seaport, later called 'Bone' and now 'Annaba', in Algeria.

[1]*'Our hearts are restless till they rest in thee'* finds echoes in the teaching of the Swiss psychologist and believer in a future existence, Carl Jung (1875–1961).
[2]*'Perfect freedom'* means free from sin, idolatry and slavery to this world's goods and temptations.

Alcuin

Almighty and merciful God, the fountain of all goodness, thou knowest the thoughts of our hearts; we confess we have sinned against thee, and done evil in thy sight. Wash us, we beseech thee, from the strains of past sins, and give us grace and power to put away hurtful things; that, being delivered from the bondage of sin, we may bring forth fruits worthy of repentance, and at last enter into thy promised joy; through the mercy of thy blessed Son Jesus Christ our Lord.

Give us grace, O Lord, to be in all things strong, prudent and just with a wise restraint at need. Grant me an exact faith, unshakeable trust in thee, and perfect charity. Fill me with the spirit of intelligence and wisdom. Let me be always thoughtful for others and courageous, with loyalty and reverence. O Light, perfect, eternal, enlighten me.

*

Alcuin (720–805). This great Yorkshire scholar and monk was made head of Charlemagne's missionary school at Aix-la-Chapelle (Aachen). There, he trained missionaries to go to the far corners of Charlemagne's empire to preach the gospel in Spain and on the borders of eastern Europe and Scandinavia.

At Aachen, he became powerful in church and state. It is not clear to what extent he influenced Pope Leo III in his decision to crown Charlemagne in Rome with the iron crown in 800 as Holy Roman Emperor when Charlemagne went there to aid Leo against his enemies. But this act was clearly premeditated, following discussions at Charlemagne's headquarters in Germany.

This event also marked the beginning of Christendom in the west and established the precedent that gave the Pope the right to confer the Imperial crown. Pope Leo was made a saint in 1673. The Holy Roman Empire lasted for 1000 years until 1800.

The monk Alcuin assists as Pope Leo III crowns Charlemagne 'Holy Roman Emperor' 800 AD.

115

St Richard of Chichester

St Richard of Chichester, with his chalice.

Thank you, Jesus Christ, for all the benefits you have given me, for all the pains and insults you have borne for me. Oh most merciful redeemer, friend and brother, may I know thee more clearly, love thee more dearly, and follow thee more nearly, day by day.

*

Saint Richard of Chichester (1197–1253). He was born Richard Wych and was a great scholar. He became chancellor to St Edmund of Abingdon at Canterbury, who had to flee to France after disagreements with King Henry III. Richard accompanied St Edmund on what was almost, for them both, a repeat of what happened to St Thomas Becket of Canterbury under Henry II, eighty years previously.

After Edmund's death in France, Richard returned to England and was elected Bishop of Chichester by the cathedral chapter. King Henry's own candidate was therefore rejected. Richard did not get possession of his see until 1246. Even then, he was not allowed the income from the cathedral lands. He, therefore, lived as a poor priest, walking daily to Chichester.

On one such occasion, while carrying the Sacraments, he dropped the cup filled with wine, but none of the wine was spilled. Throughout his brief tenure of his see, he was at his happiest with the humble people of his flock. He attacked nepotism and simony and held synods to do away with abuses.

His shrine is behind the altar in Chichester Cathedral by a fine modern tapestry and near some mosaic remains from the Roman City.

St Francis of Assisi

Lord, make me the instrument of thy peace; where there is hatred let me sow love, where there is injury let me sow pardon, where there is despair let me give hope, where there is darkness let me give light, where there is sadness let me give joy.

O Divine Master, grant that I may not try to be comforted but to comfort, not to try to be understood but to understand, not to try to be loved but to love.

Because it is in giving that we are received, it is in forgiving that we are forgiven, and it is in dying that we are born to eternal life.

O God, Creator of mankind, I do not aspire to comprehend you or your creation, nor to understand pain and suffering. I aspire only to relieve pain and suffering in others, and I trust in doing so, I may understand more clearly your nature, that you are the Father of all mankind, and that the hairs of my head are numbered.[1]

O Little Brother Bird, that brimmest with full heart, and have nought, possessest all, surely thou dost well to sing! For thou hast life without labour, and beauty without burden, and riches without care. When thou wakest, lo, it is dawn; and when thou comest to sleep it is eve. And when thy two wings are folded above thy heart, lo, there is rest. Therefore sing, Brother, having this great wealth, that when thou singest thou givest thy riches to all.

*

St Francis of Assisi (1181–1226). Patron Saint of Italy (with St Catherine of Siena); he received his 'call' in a dream in which Christ told him to 'rebuild my church'. He founded the Franciscan Order dedicated to Poverty, Charity and Penance; he preached to birds and animals, to all creation; he received the stigmata.

[1]See Matthew 10/29.

Saint Francis of Assisi:
'Make me an instrument of Thy Peace.'
(He is shown here with the wolf of Gubbio, whom he tamed.)

St Thomas Aquinas

St Thomas Aquinas has a mystical experience of the Truth & Joy beyond this life.

Grant me, I beseech Thee, Almighty and most merciful God, fervently to desire, wisely to search out, and perfectly to fulfil all that is well-pleasing unto Thee. Order thou my worldly condition to the glory of Thy name; and, of all that thou requirest me to do, grant me the knowledge, the desire, the ability, that I may so fulfil it, and may my path to thee, I pray, be safe, straightforward and perfect to the end.

Give me, O Lord, a steadfast heart which no unworthy thought can drag downwards; an unconquered heart which no tribulation can wear out; an upright heart which no unworthy purpose may tempt aside. Bestow upon me also, O Lord my God, understanding to know thee, diligence to seek thee, wisdom to find thee, and a faithfulness that may finally embrace thee; through Jesus Christ, our Lord.

*

St Thomas Aquinas (1224–1274). The greatest Catholic scholar of the Middle Ages. His prolific writings systematised the newly rediscovered works of Aristotle into the Latin theology.[1] Following Aristotle, he taught that the human soul was essentially embodied in us (cf Carl Jung, 1875–1961, who believed this in our own time) and yet was also a spiritual substance.

As the illustration shows, towards the end of his life, St Thomas had a mystical experience of the truth and joy beyond this life, which led him to say that, in comparison, all his earlier works seemed like so much straw.

He has had a powerful influence on the thought of the Catholic church in every century since his death.

[1]Rediscovered in the West through Arabic translations.

Martin Luther

Behold, Lord, an empty vessel that needs to be filled. My Lord, fill it. I am weak in the faith; strengthen me. I am cold in love; warm me and make fervent, that my love may go out to my neighbour. I do not have a strong and firm faith; at times I doubt and am unable to trust you altogether. O Lord, help me. Strengthen my faith and trust in you.

O God, whose name is holy of itself, we pray that it may be hallowed also by us. To this end help us, O blessed Father in heaven, that thy word may be taught in truth and purity, and that we, as thy children, may lead holy lives in accordance with it; through Jesus Christ, thy Son, our Lord. Amen.

*

Martin Luther (1483–1546). When Luther nailed his challenge to the papacy on Wittenburg church door, he lit the fuse for the Reformation. The Pope's raising of funds by selling 'indulgences' offended his conviction that 'Man is justified by faith alone, not by works', least of all by 'works' bought for cash. Disgust with papal morals and loose doctrine and insistence on papal supremacy, despite the new knowledge and ideas of the Renaissance, had long been growing. Vernacular translations of the Bible helped this. For the next three centuries, 'Protestant' scholars led the field in critical examination of the Scriptures. Luther's own German translation of the Bible is one of the glories of that language.

Martin Luther nailing his 95 Theses to the door of All Saints Church, Wittenburg 1517

The Just Man lives by Faith alone

'The just man lives by faith alone.'

St John Fisher

Thou knowest, good Lord, my tribulation, and now I am turned to thee; why sufferest thou me so long to be vexed with this trouble? Calm the winds, assuage the tempests, deliver my soul from these storms, for if thy meekness be turned to me, and thou look upon me, all the members of my body, and also my soul shall rest in peace. Therefore, good Lord, be thou turned to me, and deliver my soul from this tribulation wherewith it is troubled by reason of my sinfulness.

*

St John Fisher (1469–1535). Bishop of Rochester. In despair at the morals of Rome, he said: 'If the Pope does not reform his court, God will find a means of doing it for him.'

Nevertheless, he could not bring himself to accept the challenges of the Protestants of many hues to the 'one and only true church'. For him, the doctrine of 'transubstantiation' was sacrosanct – the Lord's Supper was not just an act of remembrance filled with deep spiritual overtones, as English reformers argued.

Finally, when King Henry VIII, for political and personal reasons, broke with Rome, and by the Act of Supremacy made himself head of the church in England, Fisher refused to obey. He was condemned to death and beheaded for 'treason', the execution taking place just as his cardinal's hat reached Dover from the Pope.

Other martyrs for conscience sake and for the Catholic church followed him to the scaffold – Sir Thomas More and, in later reigns, many more, of whom two groups of 54 and 80 have since been canonised as saints.

Martyrdom of St John Fisher, Bishop of Rochester 1535.

Thomas Cranmer

Almighty and everlasting God, who hatest nothing that thou hast made, and dost forgive the sins of all them that are truly penitent; create and make in us new and contrite hearts that we, worthily lamenting our sins, and acknowledging our wretchedness, may obtain of thee, the God of all mercy, perfect remission and forgiveness, through Jesus Christ our Lord.

O Lord, who has taught us that all our doings without charity are nothing worth; send thy Holy Spirit, and pour into our hearts that most excellent gift of charity, the very bond of peace and of all virtues, without which whosoever liveth is counted dead before thee: Grant us this for thine only Son Jesus Christ's sake.

*

Thomas Cranmer (1489–1556). First Archbishop of Canterbury of the reformed Church of England. Martyred in reign of Mary. From 1520, he was attracted by Luther's revolt against Rome – discussed the new ideas with William Tyndale, translator of the Bible into English – made Archbishop by Henry VIII in 1533. He shaped the Church of England, producing the Prayer Books of 1549 & 1552 and the basis for the '30 Articles' in Edward VI's reign. He supported the protestant Lady Jane Grey as Queen instead of the Roman Catholic Mary. Arrested for treason in 1553.

He was forced to witness the burning for heresy of Nicholas Ridley, Bishop of London, and Hugh Latimer, former bishop of Worcester, at Oxford 1555. Torture forced him to recant but, defiant at the stake, he withdrew his recantation, declaring that Transubstantiation was untrue and that the Pope's powers had been usurped. He thrust his right hand, which had signed his recantation, into the flames saying: *'If thy right hand offend thee, strike it off'* (Mark 9/43). At the stake the year before, Latimer had said: *'Be of good cheer Master Ridley, and play the*

Thomas Cranmer 1489–1556.

man; we shall this day light a candle by God's grace in England as I trust shall never be put out.' All three martyrs took the view of the early church Fathers, as expressed by Ratrumnus, the learned opponent of St Paschasius Radbertus, originator of the doctrine of Transubstantiation in the mid 9th century, that the Sacraments were only symbolically Christ's Body and Blood and not actually so.

St Ignatius of Loyola

Teach us, good Lord, to serve you as you deserve; to give and not to count the cost; to fight and not to heed the wounds; to toil and not to ask for any reward, save that of knowing that we do your will; through Jesus Christ our Lord.

Fill us, we pray, Lord, with your light and life that we may show forth your wondrous glory. Grant that your love may so fill our lives that we may count nothing too small to do for you, nothing too much to give and nothing too hard to bear.

*

Saint Ignatius of Loyola (1491–1556). A key figure in the Counter-Reformation which Pope Paul III initiated at the Council of Trent (Trento, Italy, 1545–63). Ignatius was a Basque Nobleman and soldier who received his call to God in a dream 'to be the servant of Christ'. Paul III allowed him to found the Society of Jesus in 1540, later known as the 'Jesuits'. The Jesuits became missionaries throughout Europe and the world and gained great influence in Church and State and in schools.

The Council of Trent, meeting under three different Popes, confirmed the basic dogmas of the Catholic Church and approved the Missal as a replacement for the multitude of 'offices' that existed prior to the Reformation and various administrative reforms. It confirmed the *'real presence'*, NOT symbolic, at the Eucharist.

On the vital issue of Justification by 'Faith alone', the Council declared: *'Only after his cooperation with the gratuitous divine assistance is man inwardly justified (acquitted) by sanctifying faith, which makes him capable of meriting good works.'*

Clearly, the Protestants had gained a point, though it was not until 1987 that the Anglo-Roman-Catholic-International-Commission (ARCIC) announced that *'we are agreed on the essential aspects of the doctrine of salvation and on the church's role within it'*.

St Ignatius of Loyola being given leave to found the Society of Jesus by Pope Paul III in 1540.

122

Sir Francis Drake

Oh Lord God, when thou givest to thy servant to endeavour any great matter, grant us also to know that it is not the beginning, but the continuing of the same to the end, until it be thoroughly finished which yieldeth the true glory; through him for who the finishing of the work laid down his life, our Redeemer, Jesus Christ.

Sir Francis Drake & The 'Golden Hind' (1587) as he proclaims his prayer before sailing to Cadiz to destroy the Spanish fleet which was being prepared to invade England and restore the Catholic faith.

Sir Francis Drake (1543–1596). His prayer symbolises the devout spirit of the Protestant faithful, their determination to seek the truth on their own, to explore and to interpret the Scriptures as the Spirit led and inspired them, as well as to fight for that cause. His inspiration here is from St Luke's gospel:

'No one who puts his hand to the plough and looks back is fit for the kingdom of God.' (Luke 9/62)

Archbishop Laud

Oh most gracious Father, we humbly beseech thee for thy Holy catholic church. Fill it with all truth; in all truth with all peace. Where it is corrupt, purge it; where it is in error, direct it; where anything is amiss, reform it; where it is right, strengthen and confirm it; where it is in want, furnish it; where it is divided, heal it and unite it in thy love; through Jesus Christ our Lord.

Grant, Lord, that we may live in your fear, die in your favour, rest in your peace, rise in your power and reign in your glory; for your own beloved Son's sake, Jesus Christ our Lord.

*

Archbishop William Laud (1573–1645). He became supreme in church and state in the reign of Charles I. He was severe on the Puritans, thus undermining the broad basis established for the Reformed English Church under Queen Elizabeth. He did, however, consider that theological disputes should be settled, as to matters of faith, by a council of the best judges. He also, against the more extreme views of some anti-catholic sections of the church, declared that the Roman Catholic Church was indeed a 'true Church'.

He replaced the Protestant pulpit, favoured by the reformed clergy, with the communion table as the main feature in anglican churches.

His fatal mistake was political, he identified the church with one party only, the King's. His trial and condemnation to death by beheading was a political murder.

*

Before his execution, Laud wrote this prayer:

'Lord, I am coming as fast as I can. I know I must pass through the shadow of death, before I come to Thee. But it is but a mere shadow, a little darkness upon nature; but Thou, by Thy merits and passion, hast broken through the jaws of death. So Lord, receive my soul, and have mercy upon me; and bless this kingdom with peace and plenty, and with brotherly love and charity, for Jesus Christ His Sake, if it be Thy will.

John Wesley

On thee we cast our care; we live through thee, who knowest our every need; oh feed us with thy grace and give our souls this day the living bread. Amen

*

Fix thou our steps, O Lord, that we stagger not at the uneven motions of the world, but steadily go on to our glorious home; neither censuring our journey by the weather we meet with, nor turning out of the way for anything that befalls us.

The winds are rough, and our own weight presses us downwards. Reach forth, O Lord, thy hand, thy saving hand, and speedily deliver us.

Teach us, O Lord, to use this transitory life as pilgrims returning to their beloved home.

*

John Wesley (1701–91) and Charles Wesley (1707–88), were both clergymen of the Church of England who had founded the 'Holy Club'. The members of the club were nicknamed 'Bible Moths' or 'Methodist' which became the name of the Church founded by the brothers. In 1735, the brothers went to Georgia in America to convert the Indians and founded the first Methodist Society.

After returning to England, unhappy with his own sense of conviction, John, aided by a Moravian group and Luther's teachings, at last experienced a deep sense of conversion and of being 'saved' through faith alone from 'sin and death'. 'An assurance was given me that Christ had taken away MY sins, even MINE.'

After John's conversion, he and his brother evangelised hundreds of thousands of the masses in the growing new industrial towns whom the other churches had failed to reach. Open air rallies, sermons and hymns and John's powerful convictions brought conversion, rebirth.

The Wesley Brothers in Georgia, 1736
'Soldiers of Christ arise!'

Their Methodist Societies believed in the Creeds and the Trinity and in Holy Communion after due preparation, but the split with the Church of England grew near.

The split came when, to Charles' sadness, for he was more orthodox than John, John Wesley ordained his own clergy to take the gospel and 'Methodism' to America.

Cardinal John Henry Newman

'Lead kindly light.'

Lead, Kindly Light, amid the encircling gloom, lead thou me on!
The night is dark, and I am far from home; lead thou me on!
Keep thou my feet; I do not ask to see the distant scene;
One step enough for me.

I was not ever thus, nor prayed that thou shouldst lead me on.
I loved to choose and see my path; but now lead thou me on.
I loved the garish day, and, spite of fears, pride ruled my will!
Remember not past years!

So long Thy power hast blest me, sure it still will lead me on,
O'er moor and fen, o'er crag and torrent, till the night is gone;
And with the morn those angel faces smile which I have loved long since,
And lost awhile.

*

John Henry Newman (1801–90). He transformed the Church of England as leader of the 'Tractarian' movement in Oxford in the 1830s, by showing the importance of the teaching of the early Fathers of the Church, like St Augustine of Hippo. But, in 1840, he shocked his followers by his 'Tract 90' which tried to show that the '39 articles' of the Church of England were consistent with the discussions of the 16th century Catholic Council of Trent.

He gave up his living of St Mary's Oxford and, in 1845, became a Roman Catholic. He was later ordained and became a Cardinal in 1879. All his life, he upheld the belief in the concept that doctrine should be a developing theological process. Through this, he persuaded the Catholic hierarchy to be reconciled to the ideas of the 'higher criticism' of the Scriptures carried out since the mid 18th century, chiefly by German Scholars. At Birmingham, Newman founded the Oratorians.

He suffered in both Anglican and Catholic churches for his views. He went through a 'dark night of the soul' of depression and doubt. His poem, the 'Dream of Gerontius', describes a soul's experience in death and was set to music by Elgar. His influence on Catholic thought resulted in his being referred to as 'The Father of the Second Vatican Council' of 1962. The Council was called by Pope John XXIII to adapt the Church to present day needs and to invite the 'separated brethren' of East and West to join in a search for reunion. In January 1991 the Pope declared Newman 'Venerable' – the first step to sainthood.

Pastor Dietrich Bonhoeffer (1916–1945)

In me there is darkness, but with you there is light, I am lonely, but you do not leave me.

I am feeble in heart, but with you there is help. I am restless, but with you there is peace.

In me there is bitterness, but with you there is patience; I do not understand your ways, but you know the way for me.

Reinhold Niebhur (1892–1971)

O God, who has bound us together in this bundle of life, give us grace to understand how our lives depend on the courage, the industry, the honesty and the integrity of our fellow men; that we may be mindful of their needs, grateful for their faithfulness and faithful in our responsibilities to them; through Jesus Christ our Lord.

*

Pastor Bonhoeffer. In this scene, Bonhoeffer represents the suffering millions in the XXth century wars and political and religious repressions. He went to his death, saying the words beneath the picture, having conducted a last service for his fellow-prisoners.

Reinhold Niebuhr. A minister of the Evangelical Synod of North America, whose writings and lectures helped to advance the 'Crisis Theology' of the 1920s and post-World War II. The crisis is the alleged failure of the church as our secular society deifies its material achievements and fails to put them to good use. The theology is too liberal for most believers but it has stimulated the debate about God.

'This is the end; for me the beginning of Life.'
Pastor Dietrich Bonhoeffer, 1945, as he was about to be executed for resisting Hitler.

127

Prayer by His Holiness Pope John-Paul II

Pope John-Paul II (Born 1920): The Pope has advanced greatly the cause of religious and political freedom, for which he was shot and badly wounded in 1981. History may well conclude that his efforts for Poland may have been crucial in breaking the weakest link in the 'Iron Curtain'. His and Archbishop Runcie's attempts to bring the Roman Catholic and Anglican Churches into 'Communion' with each other have made progress over theological issues about the Eucharist and 'Authority', but they have stalled temporarily over the ordination of women. However, both Churches know there is no going back – unity is the long-term aim.[1,2]

The Pope's efforts for cooperation and 'unity' of purpose, in its widest sense, advanced dramatically at Assisi on October 27th 1986, when he held a Day of Fasting and Prayer for Peace. He stood side by side with the Archbishop, Dr Runcie, the Dalai Lama, the Greek Orthodox Archbishop from England and leaders of most Christian denominations and from the Jewish, Muslim, Hindu, Sikh, Buddhist, Bahai, Taoist and other faiths. No better place could have been chosen than this one, where St Francis received his call to 'rebuild my church'.

[1] Even on the ordination of women, the RC church may be making some progress. Pope Paul VI, in 1976, made St Teresa of Avila (1515–1582) a 'Doctor of the Church', and therefore a 'Teacher' of the Faith. Women can also now be Ministers of the Host to Catholics.
[2] The work of the Anglican Roman Catholic International Committee is crucial in this work, which still goes on.

A Prayer for Unity between the Churches, given at Canterbury Cathedral on June 29th 1982

O Christ, may all that is part of today's encounter be born of the Spirit of truth and be fruitful through love.

Behold before us: the past and the future. Behold before us: the desires of so many hearts.

You, who are the Lord of history and the Lord of human hearts, be with us, Christ Jesus, eternal Son of God, be with us. Amen

A Prayer for the Family

Lord God, from you every family on earth takes its name. Father, you are Love and Life. Through your Son, Jesus Christ, born of woman, and through your Holy Spirit, foundation of divine charity, grant that every family on earth may become for each successive generation a true shrine of life and love.

Grant that your grace may guide the thoughts and actions of husbands and wives for the good of their families and of the families of this world. Grant that the young may find in the family solid support for their human dignity and for their growth in truth and love.

Grant that love, strengthened by the grace of sacrament of marriage, may prove mightier than all the weaknesses and trials through which our families seem to pass. Through the intercession of the Holy Family of Nazareth, grant that the Church may fruitfully carry out her world-wide mission in the family and through the family.

We ask this of you, who are the Life, the Truth, and the Way, with the Son and the Holy Spirit. Amen

Pope John-Paul II at Coventry, June 1982
'Let us build a Cathedral of Peace.'

A Prayer by Dr Robert Runcie, Lord Runcie of Cuddesdon, Archbishop of Canterbury, 1980–1991

Eternal Father, source of life and light, whose love extends to all people, all creatures, all things; Grant us that Reverence for Life which become those who believe in you, lest we despise it, degrade it, or come callously to destroy it. Rather let us save it, secure it, sanctify it after the example of your son, Jesus Christ, Our Lord.

REVERENCE FOR LIFE, as it is expressed in the Archbishop's prayer, applies to the whole of God's creation, but especially to all living creatures. He reminds us that the light which God brought out of darkness at the time of the creation and which Our Lord brought to us, 'the people that lived in darkness', was based on love.

Love is the very corner-stone of Our Lord's teaching, and 'Reverence for Life' is the doctrine of 'Love thy neighbour as thyself' expressed in cosmic terms. Albert Schweitzer[1] pointed this out when he coined the phrase of reverence for life in 1915, as he sailed up the Ogowe river in Gabon to visit a sick patient. It was brought into his mind by the sight of the antediluvian scenes of animal and bird life on either bank of the river. This made him realise that, to the creator, all creation is sacred and should be revered.

This experience helped him to sum up his own observations of life and find how close they were also to his own religious convictions. For Schweitzer, 'Reverence for Life', became a way of Life – 'Love in action'.

By making this phrase the keystone of his prayer, the Archbishop has added a new dimension of the church's store of prayers. He has done it at a time when the world is most in need of this new and original source of religious inspiration – not least because mankind and the environment are in danger from our invention and material waste. If we think about it, we can see that reverence for life can be applied as a theme for improving and for protecting every value and every worthwhile human activity. It could reach across the barriers that divide races and creeds. If adopted widely enough as a principle of living – of love – all peoples and all faiths could rally to its banner. In this way, they would help themselves and each other by sharing in suffering and in joy and in effort, to make life richer, more beautiful, happier for all.

Above all, this reverence for life could lead to a great spiritual revival in a world that has become too material and too boastful of its own inventions. There are hopeful signs, so far chiefly based on fear of extinction, but also on love. The peoples of the world are at last paying serious attention to saving and securing, even sanctifying, the environment and nature in general.

We shall know when this cult has really taken root, for it will be seen in the field of visual arts, just as movingly as it was centuries ago in the age of faith, when our great cathedrals (also the great mosques and other religious buildings) were created. His Royal Highness, the Prince of Wales, mentioned this point when he spoke to the American Architects at their gathering in February 1990. He then said that he hoped – *'we might strive for an age of reverence – reverence for what gave us life and for the fragile world in which we live'.*

[1]*Dr Albert Schweitzer 1875–1965.* Medical missionary, theologian organist and expert on Bach. Author of 'The Quest for Historical Jesus' and other works, including 'My Life and Thought'.

Eternal Father, source of Life and Light whose Love extends to all people, all creatures, all things: grant us that Reverence for Life which becomes those who believe in you, Lest we despise it, degrade it, or come callously to destroy it. Rather let us save it, secure it and sanctify it after the example of your Son Jesus Christ Our Lord.
Robert Runcie

'Grant us reverence for life.'

Epilogue

'The debate about God is still the most important question
confronting humankind today'[1]

STORY-TELLER: In the picture, we show people from many different races and faiths. They are all travelling together through life as pilgrims. In the distance is a symbolic goal – the Kingdom, though this is a spiritual goal rather than a geographical location. Some of the pilgrims are on the road from apathy or unbelief to belief in Jesus – some represent the different Christian denominations as they move towards unity – the rest are followers of the other world religions.

INTERPRETER: It is right to show Christians and people from other faiths in this way because, as the Doctrine Commission has written, they are allies – *'in the sense that they are engaged in the same enterprise. They too are attempting to "read" the universe, to evaluate their experience, in the light of an inherited tradition. We believe that the Christian revelation is true in many ways in which theirs is false. But there is much in Christian and other traditions which overlaps – enough to suggest that all are in touch in some degree with a single reality which, in these different idioms, is acknowledged and worshipped as God.'*[2]

STORY-TELLER: The Doctrine Commission goes on to say that these other faiths *'can become part of the resources of reason and experience which help to make explicit the doctrine of God implied in our own Scripture and tradition; and this should lead us to show openness and reverence towards the beliefs and practices of others'.* A dialogue with them on equal terms need not imply *'indifference to the question of the truth and the uniqueness of the Christian revelation, but it can greatly widen our view of the resources available to interpret and explore that revelation, and of the human potential which that revelation may be able to release'.*[3]

INTERPRETER: This kind of dialogue could succeed in bringing theologians, priests, scientists, scholars, philosophers and ordinary people of every faith closer together. They could then seek to interpret jointly the spiritual significance of the many great discoveries that will be made in the 21st century after the Birth of Jesus Christ. Some of these discoveries, probably based on research now being undertaken, could widen and deepen our knowledge of the universe, of ourselves and even of the very mind of God.

STORY-TELLER: The Christian approach to this need not be a threat to the traditions of others. This is because, though Jesus said *'I am the Way the Truth and the Life'*,[4] his way is through love. That is to say, through love of God and love of our neighbour. We can therefore rely on him – through faith, hope and love and the gift of the Holy Spirit – to guide us all.

INTERPRETER: It may help if we now outline some of the points where Christian and other traditions overlap and where the present lines of demarcation exist.

Most other faiths share a common belief with Christians in God the Creator, and also in a divinely inspired moral code – like the Ten Commandments, common to Jews, Christians and to followers of Islam. Most religions also believe in an ultimate day of reckoning – in rewards and punishments, and in some form of future life. Jews and Christians share the books of the Old Testament – Muslims revere the Old Testament prophets and the 'Book' – the first five 'Books of Moses'.

The Koran even praises the Gospel, while condemning the squabbles about the nature of God, which caused so much strife between the many Christian sects of Mahomet's day and previously. The Koran also declares that God sent his Spirit to create Jesus in Mary's womb,

[1]See 'We believe in God'. A Report by the Doctrine Commission of the Church of England, 1986, page 16.
[2] and [3]Ditto pages 13 and 14.
[4]John 14/6.

(continued on page 134)

132

'The way to the kingdom.'

133

though Mahomet could not bring himself to accept Jesus as Son of God, but only as a prophet. The Jewish, Christian and Muslim faiths all believe in God's Spirit – and, in essence, the Holy Spirit of the Christian faith and the Spirit of Yahweh for the Jews are one and the same.

STORY-TELLER: We cannot tell how far we are along the road to the Kingdom – except that the world is patently not yet ready, morally or spiritually, for God's rule on Earth. In one sense, however, we are not only 'pilgrims' but also 'inheritors' of the Kingdom, since Jesus said – *'the Kingdom of God is within you'*, (or, *'in the midst of you'*).[1]

This seems to imply that the Kingdom is an inward reality that is latent within us – or that it actually began with his own ministry – or that it is present in the universal Church and is being developed through the gift of the Holy Spirit. It could mean all three of these possibilities. In any case, it does seem, from our experience since biblical times, that we are still only at the beginning of the pilgrimage towards the fulfilment of the Kingdom – God's rule on earth.

PRIEST: Let us sum up by saying that we can have the confidence – through Jesus' promises to us – that the Kingdom will be achieved and that he will come to us again – and that he will fulfil the words of the prophets – as he said he would. Therefore one day – far in the future – a day will come when:– *'Every valley will be lifted up, every mountain and hill will be laid low, the uneven ground will become level and the rough places a plain. And the glory of the LORD shall be revealed and all flesh shall see it together.'*[2]

But we must also remember: *'Watch therefore, for you know neither the day nor the hour.'*[3]

Let us end with these two prayers – one for ourselves and one for unity in the universal Church – that unity which Dr Robert Runcie, as Archbishop of Canterbury, described on his return from seeing the Pope in Rome as: *'unity in all its rich diversity'*.[4]

O God, please grant that your spirit will inspire me and give me strength to achieve one good thing each day towards advancing that Kingdom for which you taught us to pray through your son, Jesus Christ, Our Lord, Amen. (Author's prayer)

'Lord God, we thank you for calling us into the company of those who trust in Christ and seek to obey his will. May your Spirit guide and strengthen us in mission and service to your world; for we are strangers no longer, but pilgrims together on the Way to your Kingdom.' Amen. (Ecumenical prayer)

[1]Luke 17/21. See also page 83 above.
[2]Isaiah 40/4 & 5.
[3]Matthew 25/13.
[4]BBC TV2 October 8th 1989.

The End

The Pilgrim's Badge.

The Missions and Dates of the Old Testament Prophets

Amos Mission *c.*790–750 BC ⎫ They had missions to Israel before its
Hosea Mission *c.*760–730 BC ⎬ defeat in 721 BC.

Isiah Lived *c.*760–690 BC. He taught Judah before the exile. His great but unknown disciple and later follower continued in his style during the exile, according to most commentators.

Micah Lived *c.*740–690 BC. His Mission was to Judah.

Jeremiah[1] Mission to Judah from *c.*640–587 BC, when he was exiled to Egypt.

Zephania Mission to Judah *c.*730–720 BC.

Ezekiel Mission *c.*590–520 BC ⎫ Returned with exiles to Jerusalem from
Haggai Mission *c.*590–520 BC ⎬ Babylon with Cyrus' permission.

Daniel Mission *c.*550–530 BC. His mission to Babylonian and Persian rulers.

Malachi Mission *c.*455–440 BC. He recalled the people to their true religious priorities after their return from exile to Jerusalem.

Joel His mission took place in about 530 BC. He proclaimed the new life that would come in the 'Last Days'.

Obadiah Mission *c.*595–570 BC. To Israel's ancient enemy Edom, around Petra.

Jonah (See mention in II Kings (14/25)). His mission may have been about 760 BC, to Nineveh. The Old Testament story about him seems to have been written in post-exilian times.

Nahum Mission *c.*630 BC. Like Jonah, his mission was to Nineveh.

[1] Jeremiah also wrote 'Lamentations'.

The Earliest Christian Documents & the Dates & Authorship of the Gospels

The Earliest Christian Documents in the Bible

St Paul's 1st Letter to the Thessalonians about 50–51 AD
St Paul's 1st Letter to the Corinthians *c*.56 AD

The Gospels   Most, but not all, scholars believe there was a collection of Jesus' sayings, now lost, that existed as a 'Source', named 'Quelle' in German, or 'Q', from which the three Evangelists, Matthew, Mark and Luke, obtained much of their gospels.

Because these three gospels give the same account for many events in almost the same words, they have been called the 'Synoptic gospels', i.e. they were written from the 'same point of view'.

St Mark   The earliest gospel, written about 64/70 AD, though some scholars say it was written much earlier. In the Early Church, there was a strong tradition that this gospel was largely dictated to Mark by St Peter. St Mark first appears as St Paul's companion in Acts. (See Acts 12/25).

St Matthew   His gospel was probably written about 80–85 AD. Matthew was a tax-collector who became a disciple. He used 'Q', like Mark. An Early Church tradition held that he obtained his 'Birth Stories' either from Joseph himself or from 'James', referred to as Jesus' 'Brother', but more probably his step-brother or cousin in the extended family circle. James became head of the church in Jerusalem and was a late convert.

St Luke   He may have written his gospel in about 90–95 AD. It has also been suggested that, despite the opening paragraphs of 'The Acts of the Apostles', also by Luke, he may have written Acts first before his gospel. The reason for this is that Acts ends on a hopeful note, making no reference to the martyrdoms of St Peter and St Paul. These took place in the reign of Nero in about 67 AD (though Acts 20/25 may refer to this). Luke was certainly St Paul's companion 'the beloved physician'.

Early tradition held that Luke obtained his birth stories from the Virgin Mary. He certainly says in his introductory paragraph to his gospel that he obtained his information from 'eye-witnesses', and later on he twice says that 'Mary kept all these things in her heart', as though he knew this from her direct.

Luke may have lived in Bithynia (NW Turkey), about 200 miles from Ephesus, where the Virgin Mary is believed, according to tradition, to have lived in the care of St John (following Jesus' last instructions on the cross). This would mean that Luke could easily have visited Mary to talk about Jesus' early life.

St John   He probably wrote his gospel in old age between 90–100 AD. He seems to have been a mere youth when he became a disciple. In his gospel, he calls himself (it seems) 'the disciple whom Jesus loved'. When his gospel was accepted into the new Testament canon in the late 2nd or early 3rd century, it was held officially that 'John' was the brother of James and also a son of Zebedee. The same tradition makes him the author of the Letters of John and of the 'Revelation to John', despite differences in style.

A Note on the Doctrine of the Holy Trinity

Introduction The Christian concept of God is of a Trinity – Three persons in one God – Father, Son and Holy Spirit – distinguishable only by number, and inseparable in their activity. We have already indicated this, together with the definition of the nature of Jesus – wholly divine and wholly human – on pages 43, 47 and 113. But more needs to be said about this 4th century doctrine, since it differs from the Jewish and Muslim definitions of God, and also because it has been suggested by some Christian scholars that this traditional definition should perhaps be changed or even abandoned. Their reason for putting these ideas forward derives from their anxiety to bridge the gap between Christianity and these other faiths.

The Attempt to Define God God is almost indefinable. The Jewish 'Yahweh' means 'I exist' or 'I am Existence itself' – a thought-provoking, deep philosophical concept. The Jews also acknowledge that the Lord God communicates with us through the 'Spirit of Yahweh'. This is, for all practical purposes, identical with the Christian notion of the Holy Spirit. To the Muslims, God is usually 'the Compassionate, the Merciful' or 'Maker of the Heavens and of the Earth'. They also recognise God's Spirit.

All of these are consistent with the attributes given to God by Christians – Almighty, Father, Maker of Heaven and Earth. The Jews cannot, however, accept that Jesus is Christ, their promised Messiah. Nor can the Muslims accept Jesus other than as a great prophet – born through a Virginal conception, of Mary and God's Holy Spirit – but whose crucifixion they regard as bogus. According to them, Jesus did not die on the cross. They cannot even accept the idea of God having a son, or of the Trinity – to them 'God is One not Three'.

The Christian definition, made in the 4th century BC, at the Councils of Nicea in 325 and of Constantinople in 381, arose from the need to defend the orthodox view of Jesus from the heresy of an Alexandrian monk called Arius. He maintained – and large numbers of bishops agreed with him – that Jesus was not born the Son of God but was only raised to 'Sonship' at his baptism, on account of his perfect goodness.

The Council of Nicea was summoned by the Emperor Constantine, 12 years after he had declared Christianity to be the official religion of the Roman Empire. He wanted this theological disagreement over Jesus settled. The council agreed on the definition of the Trinity and the nature of Jesus, exiled Arius and deposed the heretical bishops. This definition was then applied to the Nicean Creed – and, later, at the Council of Constantinople, to the Athanasian creed, St Athanasius having been a moving light on the side of orthodoxy.

This was not the end of the matter. Arian missionaries took their heretical version elsewhere, when they crossed the Danube to convert the eastern tribes. These later took their heresy with them, when they invaded the west. The heresy was not eliminated in Lombardy until almost the 8th century. It still exists in one form, in the view taken of Jesus by Jehovah's Witnesses.

The Trinity Today and in the Future As we have indicated earlier, the Doctrine of the Trinity is implicit in the gospels and in the Christian experience of God in countless spiritual encounters since then. For those Christians, therefore, who feel the need for the abandonment or redefining of the doctrine, these words, written to the author by the Reverend Basil Watson,[1] may be helpful:– *'What is important to me in the doctrine of the Trinity is its guarantee that God the Father is exactly as we see Him in Jesus. We think all too easily that God Almighty – the Father – acts differently from Jesus. For me both act in the same spirit. Experience also dictates the need of the doctrine – the mystery – before which we acknowledge our humble understandings.'*

[1]See under 'Acknowledgements'.